PAPER TALK

ILLUSTRATED LETTERS OF CHARLES M. RUSSELL

Introduction and Commentary by FREDERIC G. RENNER

AMON CARTER MUSEUM OF WESTERN ART

FORT WORTH, TEXAS

The Amon Carter Museum of Western Art, established under the will of the late Amon G. Carter, is concerned with the study and documentation of the American West. The program of the Museum is expressed in publications and exhibitions related to the many aspects of American culture which find their identification as "western."

Cover Photograph of CHARLES M. RUSSELL
by DOROTHEA LANGE

CHARLES M. RUSSELL, ca. 1924. *by Dorothea Lange*

"As I look at the photograph, what I remember is the atmosphere, the light, the qualities of easy-going conversation or communication between Charlie Russell and Maynard Dixon, in whose studio it was made. I was not a participant; I was just there and the camera was with me. I saw it and I did it. Charlie Russell did not sit for me. I doubt if he knew that the picture had been made, for they were in conversation and the camera was not the reason for the visit. However, I do know that this was a serious conversation. They were not on this occasion spinning yarns, or trading anecdotes on western lore, or entertaining each other, which both of these men knew how to do very well. I seem to remember that Charlie Russell was just passing through town. I never saw him again, or heard of his being in San Francisco again.

This is the most that I can dig out of my memory today, little enough, but it was nevertheless an afternoon which has remained with me. It had a quality not unlike other rare occasions, when I have been in the presence of old-type American Indians. There is a sort of echo, which remains and is unforgettable."

DOROTHEA LANGE
NOVEMBER 30, 1961

ACKNOWLEDGMENT

This publication and the accompanying exhibition was first suggested by visitors to the Amon Carter Museum. The interest and pleasure which our guests displayed in Charlie Russell's correspondence prompted the effort to locate other letters which might complement the Museum's collection. The generous cooperation of numerous individuals and institutions has made possible the selection of 79 letters and countless photographs, programs, and cards revealing the personality of the strangely profound man, Charlie Russell.

To locate, check, and evaluate this mass of material called for the sympathetic attention of one who had known Russell. Frederic G. Renner, a Montanan by birth, knew the artist when he lived in Great Falls in the early years of this century. Fred Renner, the boy, had the extraordinary privilege of knowing Charlie and seeing him through boyhood eyes, with the excitement, noise, dust, and smells that meant a small western town in those days. Later, Renner, the man, was able to return to study the idol of his youth and start the patient, painstaking compilation of details necessary to the careful documentation of a biography. Renner worked with Charlie's widow, Nancy, with his old cronies in Montana, with art dealers in New York, with books, scrawled notes, and pictures. Without this background, the "paper talk" of Charlie Russell could not be presented as visual documentation of the man.

The Carter Museum is indebted to many friends for assistance in locating materials. Loans to the exhibition are credited individually. Of special importance is the generous cooperation of the Trustees of the C. M. Russell Gallery, Great Falls, Montana, and their President, William H. Bertsche, Jr., and the Montana State Historical Society, Helena, Montana, and the Director, Michael Kennedy. Without the loans extended from these outstanding collections of Russell material this exhibition could not have been assembled. In addition, there are the following contributors whose research and suggestions have resulted in valuable enrichment of this study.

Lee Angle
Fort Worth, Texas

Stephen A. Bollinger
Los Angeles, California

Mrs. Edward Borein
Santa Barbara, California

G. L. Bowen, General Passenger Manager
The Cunard Steam-Ship Company Limited
New York City

Carl Brueggemeyer
Pittsburgh Post-Gazette

T. B. Buchholz
The Buchholz Galleries
Bradford, Pennsylvania

Miss Helen Card
The Latendorf Bookshop
New York City

Miss Suzanne Caster
San Francisco Chronicle

Mrs. Wallace D. Coburn
Santa Barbara, California

Seymour V. Connor, Director
Southwest Collection
Texas Technological College
Lubbock, Texas

John Dewar, Curator
William S. Hart Museum
Newhall, California

John S. du Mont, O.S.J.
Greenfield, Massachusetts

Mrs. Laura Allyn Ekstrom
State Historical Society of Colorado
Denver, Colorado

Mrs. Ruth K. Field, Curator
Missouri Historical Society
St. Louis, Missouri

Dick Flood
Trailside Galleries
Idaho Falls, Idaho

Casey Foster
B.P.O.E.
Great Falls, Montana

Paul V. Francis
Office of the President
Richfield Oil Corporation
Los Angeles, California

W. Edwin Gledhill, Museum Director
The Santa Barbara Historical Society

Miss Edith Hamlin
San Francisco, California

Victor J. Hammer
Hammer Galleries
New York City

Mrs. W. H. Haws, Curator
C. M. Russell Log Cabin Studio
Great Falls, Montana

Ira Kaufman
Great Falls, Montana

Fred Kennedy
Calgary, Alberta
Canada

Miss Dorothea Lange
Berkeley, California

Robert W. Love, Manager
Will Rogers Memorial
Claremore, Oklahoma

William R. Mackay
Roscoe, Montana

Miss Ruth I. Mahood
Los Angeles County Museum

Miss Grace Mayer
Museum of Modern Art
New York City

Harold McCracken, Director
Whitney Gallery of Western Art
Cody, Wyoming

George McCue, Art News Editor
St. Louis Post-Dispatch

"The Mint"
Great Falls, Montana

Mrs. Dorothy Neuman
Central Public Library
St. Louis, Missouri

Ward S. Parker
St. Louis, Missouri

Miss Patti C. Parsons
Chouinard Art Institute
Los Angeles, California

Philip A. Rees
Museum of the City of New York

Franz R. Stenzel, M.D.
Portland, Oregon

Jack Stevenson
Attorney for the Trigg Foundation
Great Falls, Montana

Miss Lirl Treuter
Art & Music Division
Fort Worth Public Library

Mrs. Velva W. Tuohy
Secretary to the Director
Montana State Historical Society
Helena, Montana

Charles van Ravenswaay, Director
Missouri Historical Society
St. Louis, Missouri

Miss Dolores Voght
Walt Disney Productions
Burbank, California

Alexander Warden, Publisher
Great Falls Tribune-Leader

Tom Weadick
San Clemente, California

Mrs. Robb Williams, Curator
C. M. Russell Gallery
Great Falls, Montana

Irving Wills, M.D.
Santa Barbara, California

Lyle S. Woodcock
St. Louis, Missouri

CHARLES M. RUSSELL

1864 - 1926

Charlie ca. 1868. Courtesy of Ward S. Parker, St. Louis, Missouri

Charles Marion Russell was born in St. Louis, Missouri of a well-to-do family and even as a youngster displayed the two major interests that were to dominate his life. One was drawing and modeling; the other, an obsession with the West.

Charlie sketched and painted on everything — the margins of his school books, his tablets, even the sidewalk and front steps. His first art prize was won at the age of twelve. The blue ribbon he was awarded at the St. Louis County Fair suggests that even these early efforts showed some talent.

Indifferent to school, Charlie haunted the riverfront to watch the soldiers and fur-traders leaving for the upper reaches of the Missouri. He was determined to go West as soon as he could leave home. Paternal lectures having no effect, Charlie's father finally concluded the only cure was to let the boy go West, thinking the hardships would soon pall on him and he would return to settle down to his school work and eventually take his place in the family business.

A family friend's return to his Montana sheep ranch in 1880 provided the opportunity for Charlie to realize his dream. The two set out from St. Louis just four days before young Russell's sixteenth birthday. Traveling by train, stagecoach, and horseback, Charlie arrived in Montana Territory, the country that was to be his home for the next forty-six years.

The country and its people made a vivid impression on the observant youngster from the distant East. Here were the cowboys and the Indians he had heard about. Along with them were many characters he had never dreamed of; bullwhackers, missionaries, gamblers, desperados, French-Canadian rivermen in bright-colored sashes, pig-tailed Chinamen, and bearded traders and trappers in buckskin. Charlie saw them all and stored away every detail of their dress and equipment in his uncanny memory.

Charlie didn't like herding sheep. With characteristic independence he quit his first job and "threw in" with Jake Hoover, a veteran mountain man. The next two years proved one of the most valuable experiences the future artist could have had. Hoover was a professional meat-hunter, and under his guidance, Charlie learned the habits of game animals, how to "read sign", and a vast store of facts about nature that he would draw upon later in his paintings.

Young Russell's first job as a cowboy came in the spring of 1882 and, except for one short period, he worked as a horse wrangler and night herder over most of central and northern Montana for the next eleven years.

The Indians were responsible for the one interlude in Charlie's life as a cowboy. Russell had always been interested in these native Americans and, realizing that times were fast changing, knew that he would have to learn as much as he could about them before it was too late. Accordingly, late in the summer of 1888, Russell pushed north to the Bow River in Canada to visit his young friend, Sleeping Thunder, the son of the Chief of the Blood Indians. Russell lived with this band of Indians until the following March — hunting with them, joining in games of skill, listening to the stories and legends of their old men during the long winter evenings. Like his life with Jake Hoover and his years around cow camps, these months of intimate association with a tribe of the "first Americans" gave Russell an insight into his subjects that came to few artists.

Russell was painting throughout the eleven year period he was on the range, mostly for his own amusement. He gave his paintings to any friend who admired them, or sold a few when it became necessary to raise a little extra money. These early paintings were mostly in water color. It wasn't until 1885 that he completed his first important oil, a roundup scene called, "Breaking Camp". This primitive painting gave little evidence of the power Russell was to display in later years but it was described so glowingly in one of the Helena newspapers that it was sent off to St. Louis to be shown at the Art Exposition of 1886, the first significant example of his work to be exhibited outside of Montana. "Breaking Camp" is now in the collection of the Historical Society of Montana. A companion piece to this first oil, "Utica Picture," painted in 1887, is in the permanent collection of The Amon Carter Museum, Fort Worth, Texas.

By 1893, Russell had become sufficiently well known as an artist throughout Montana that he decided to devote full time to his painting.

As he put it, "That fall when work was over I left (the range) and I never sang to the horses or cows again".

Settling down in Great Falls, Russell's first studio was a back room in the Brunswick Bar owned by his friend, Albert Trigg. This was a convenient place for Charlie to meet and enjoy his friends. It also provided a place to show his paintings to an occasional customer, but this was probably of secondary importance.

A turning point in Russell's life came with his marriage to Nancy Cooper in the fall of 1896. Nancy was only eighteen but she had supreme faith in Charlie's ability and a driving ambition of her own which she set out to satisfy by helping her husband achieve success.

The rest of Russell's career as an artist is well known. He became a successful illustrator, with such famous authors as Owen Wister, Emerson Hough, and Stewart Edward White making use of his work. His paintings were widely exhibited, and sold at ever increasing prices. Long before his death in 1926, those competent to judge recognized Charles M. Russell as the pre-eminent artist of the Old West.

Russell's great ability as an artist is preserved in his paintings and sculpture. His letters provide an equally important record of the man. These reveal his friendships, his imagination and humor, his beliefs and philosophy, and help explain why Russell the man is respected and loved fully as much as Russell the artist.

Russell's letters were invariably couched in the vernacular of the Old West, which is part of their charm. Many people have been amused at his spelling and his indifference to most of the rules of grammar and punctuation. Some have conjectured, too, whether this was the result of Russell's lack of formal schooling or was deliberate on his part; a type of showmanship. It was neither. Russell was being himself, writing as he and most other Montanans of that day talked.

Charlie claimed to be "lame with a pen" and insisted that while he might be "average on talk", he was "deaf and dum with writing tools". The intimate friends who received his letters didn't share these views. Charlie could spell correctly when he wanted to but, to him, this was unimportant as long as he was understood. It was the idea behind the words that interested him. Here, Russell was a master. In all his writings the meaning was crystal-clear as the mountain streams of his beloved Rockies. Few could say so much in so few words, or say it in such an amusing fashion. Russell's letters are valued for these reasons as much as for the drawings and paintings that adorn them.

The variety of Russell's friends and the lasting quality of his friendships as revealed in his letters give us some clues to the nature of the man. Russell's friends included the frontiersmen he met in his early days in Montana, the cowboys he worked with, the Indians whose trails he crossed, gamblers and preachers, and respected business men. The fact that some of the latter were saloon keepers as well as bankers and judges had no influence on Russell's friendships. As fame grew, so, too, did his host of friends. They included nationally known artists and actors, writers, railroad presidents, and United States Senators. Russell once wrote, "I had friends when I had nothing else." His letters show that he treasured his friendships, and he never forgot one of them.

A characteristic that stands out in all of Russell's letters is his deep love for the Old West and all that it stood for as a way of life. Russell's sketch of an old-time Montana cowboy, in a letter to his friend, Wallace Coburn, and his comment that "We both knew this kind" reflected more than mere longing for the care-free days of the open range. His feelings went much deeper. Russell sensed that the frontier itself meant something important in his country's heritage. He knew that life on the frontier not only required such qualities as honesty, courage, and self-reliance. It engendered them in a man. His instincts told him that man was renewed when he lived close to nature. In Russell's mind, unlocked doors with the latch string always out, and a man's word as good as his bond, were part and parcel of this same relationship to the frontier. He called them, "the honest days", and he didn't think they would necessarily be improved with the coming of civilization. Many men of this time were aware that an era was dying and most of them were doing all they could to hasten the end. Russell was one of the few who saw, and regretted, the profound effects the change would bring to the country and its people.

Russell has been described as a tolerant man, but his letters show that he had opinions of his own. He never hesistated to express them, even when he disagreed with the popular views of the time. A pet hatred was General Sherman for the remark attributed to him, and shared by many Montanans, that "the only good Indian was a dead Indian". This view was widely held by the Army and is possibly the reason why Russell, unlike Remington, never painted the United States soldier or cavalryman as a colorful dashing figure. Russell understood and shared the Indian's love of freedom, admired their way of life, respected their religion, and had many personal friends among the Plains tribes. He was outspoken in his disapproval of their shameful treatment and had little sympathy for the popular demand that Indian lands be opened for white settlement. He ridiculed the Government attempts to make farmers of them. As he wrote his friend Harry Stanford, "once Nature gave him (the Indian) everything he wanted, now the agent gives him bib overalls, hookes his hands around plow handles, and tells him its a good thing to push, maby it is, but thair having a hell of a time prooving it".

Russell was no more sympathetic towards the hordes of white farmers who invaded his beloved Montana to "turn the grass wrong side up". He called them "punkin rollers", akin to the clods their plow-shares turned up. To Russell, the deliberate destruction of Montana's beautiful grasslands was little short of desecration. His convictions were based on more than the natural antipathy of the old-time cowman to squatters and homesteaders. He had seen the misery that followed crop failures in a land where a harsh climate and poor soils foredoomed the settler's high hopes. He also had the perception to know that once the grass was destroyed, the immemorial breeding grounds of the wild fowl would be gone, and weeds, clogged streams, and desolation would follow. Unfortunately, it was to be another half-century before many other Montanans saw the truth of his views and appealed for help to re-grass more than seven million acres that had been unwisely plowed. As a conservationist, Russell was many years ahead of his time.

He was a light-hearted man and he saw humor in everything, includ-ing himself. He loved to poke fun at the high-and-mighty, the moralist, and the self-righteous. He could demolish an ego with an apt phrase that left his listeners and the victim chuckling. Russell's humor showed in everything he did. It might come out in a painting of an over-confi-dent cowboy flying through the air from the back of a bronco, or a self-assured porcupine facing down a mighty grizzly. It appeared in the stories for which he was famous. Especially is it apparent in his letters to his intimate friends. Russell's observations were made amusing by the language in which they were expressed, but the real basis for his humor was a shrewd knowledge of nature, human and otherwise. If it was sometimes sardonic, it was always kindly.

A down-to-earth way of looking at life and an unerring instinct for what was true or false marked Russell for the philosopher that he was. As his close friend, Will Rogers put it, Charlie could *think* twice as straight as he could draw a line with a brush. Along with the originality of his observations, Russell expressed his thoughts in pungent language that even Rogers couldn't equal. Long after Rogers had become famous, when the two men got together with a group of friends, it was Charlie they demanded to hear. Will was an enraptured listener.

Irvin S. Cobb, the famous humorist, knew both men, and aside from Charlie's ability as an artist considered them much alike. Rogers was a marvelous speech-maker, and loved it. Russell hated the limelight and was at his best hunkered on his heels, a small group of friends around him, and, according to Cobb, with "wisdom seeping out like sugar dripping from a sugar tree".

His friendships, his unchanging love for the Old West, and his scorn for those who would despoil it, his regard for the Indian, his originality and insistence on being himself, his humor and wisdom — all these are in the "paper talk" of the prophetically sensitive man. C. M. Russell.

The men who knew Charlie Russell recognized these qualities and he would have been loved for the kind of a man he was had he never achieved fame as an artist. An evening with Charlie was an experience to be remembered and his letters were so prized that few of them ever passed into other hands during the recipient's lifetime.

Albert Trigg was one of those who saved every letter he received from Charlie. The Trigg home adjoined Charlie's Log Cabin Studio in Great Falls and the two men had corresponded for more than two decades. After Mr. Trigg's death, his letters were carefully preserved by his daughter, Josephine, who willed them to the people of Great Falls. They are now owned by the C. M. Russell Gallery of that city.

After Russell's death in 1926, his wife assembled nearly 150 of the letters Charlie had written to his friends over the years for the purpose of having them published. These appeared in the book, "Good Medicine" (Doubleday, 1929) for which Will Rogers wrote the foreword. Some of the letters to Albert Trigg were among those Josephine loaned to Nancy for this purpose.

Charlie also wrote many letters to his friend, Bill Rance, the proprietor of "The Silver Dollar", and to Sid Willis who owned "The Mint", the equally famous establishment directly across the street in Great Falls. As these were received, they were lovingly framed and hung in the owner's place of business to be seen and enjoyed by many of Russell's other friends.

Neither Bill Rance nor Sid Willis looked with favor on commercializing the letters by having them published in a book for public sale. Consequently, both refused to permit the ones they owned to be used for this purpose. Rance's letters were willed to the Elk's Club of Great Falls where he and Charlie were members. Those owned by Sid Willis remained in his possession as a part of the famous "Mint Collection" until a few years ago.

Frederic G. Renner

January 15, 1962
Washington, D. C.

PAPER TALK

C. M. Russell

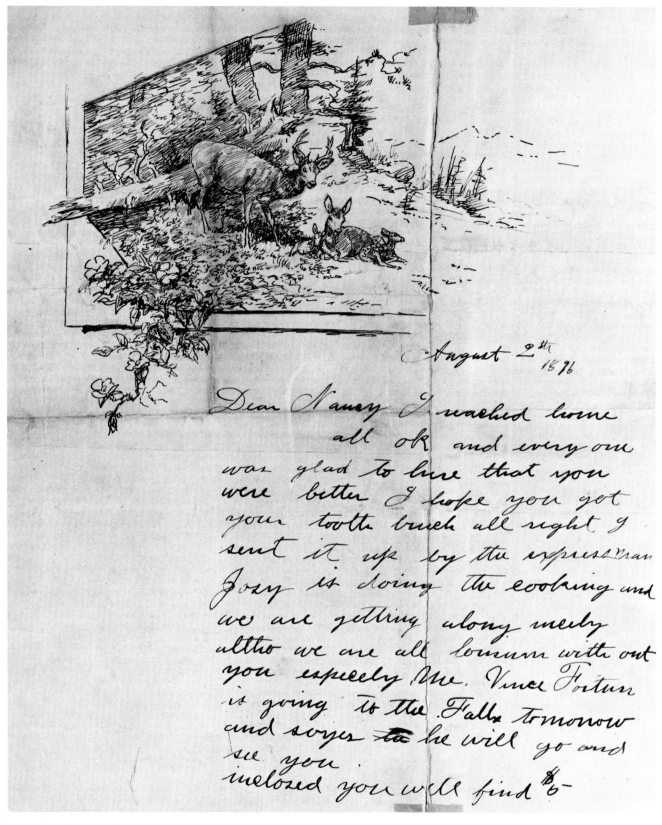

Nancy's First Love Letter

Five weeks before they were to be married, Nancy Cooper became ill and Charlie took her to Great Falls where she could receive better care. While there Charlie visited Victor Egloff, the leading jeweler of the town, to purchase her wedding ring before returning to Cascade. The amusing incident of the tooth brush is explained by the fact that it was a common practice in those days to ask the friendly expressman to deliver small articles while on his rounds. As this was Nancy's first trip away from Cascade since she had met Charlie, this was probably her first love letter from him.

Courtesy of Chas. S. Jones, Los Angeles

I thought you might need it I got the your ring all right but left it at Egloffs to have our initials put in it I think you will like it Maggy will be here to monow well as Nancy as there is no news to tell you you I will close with much love and x x x x x

I am yours truly

C M Russell

I will send the Picture to monow

"Whitetails", Watercolor by Charles M. Russell

The picture mentioned at the close of the accompanying letter was to be Charlie's first present to his bride-to-be. This was a beautiful watercolor painting of a deer family and their friends in a wooded retreat, a painting that was to hang in the Russell home until the day of Nancy's death forty-five years later.

Courtesy of F. G. Renner, Washington, D. C.

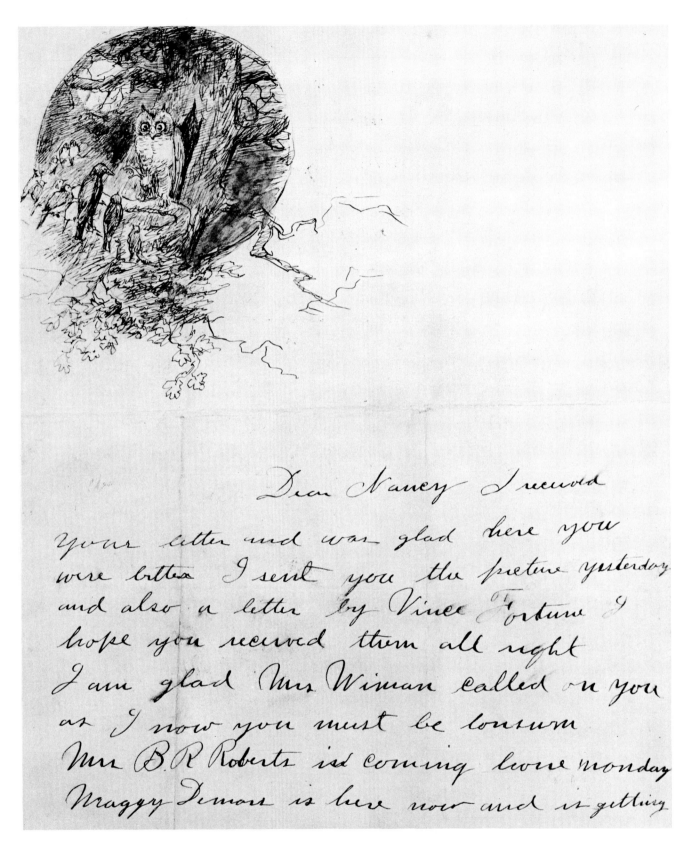

Letter to Nancy, undated (August 1896)

This letter was written to Nancy during her stay in Great Falls the month before her marriage to Charlie. Mrs. B. R. Roberts mentioned in the letter was Charlie's adopted "mother" in Cascade and the ceremony was to be held at the home of Mr. and Mrs. Roberts. As Charlie was to tell the story later, "I borrowed fifteen dollars to get married. I give five to the bunch to keep 'em from shivereein' me, five to the preacher, an' kept five to get along on. We lived on the five dollars for a year in Cascade an' our wedding trip was a hundred yards to a one-room shack—an' we walked."

meely Josy is here with us I suppose you
herd that the house caught fire but it
did not do much damage as we got it
out before it got much hed way and you
would hardly know there had been a fire
well nancy I cant write any more as
it is late and I want to get it of our
to nights mail so I will close with love
                        Yours C. M. Russell

XXXXX XX

maggy and Josey send there best love

Wedding Picture of Charles and Nancy Russell

Courtesy of F. G. Renner, Washington, D. C.

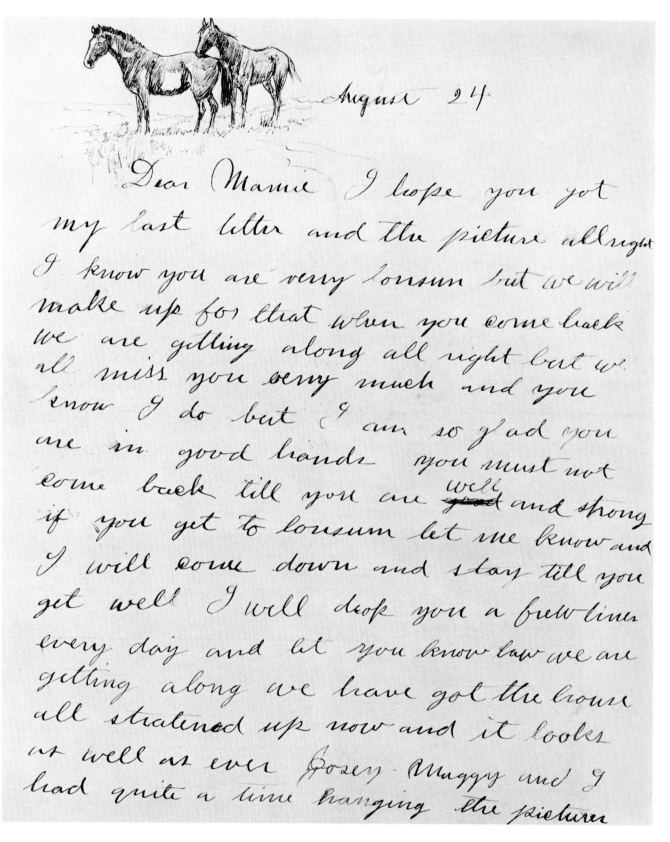

August 24

Dear Mamie I hope you got my last letter and the picture allright I know you are verry lonsum but we will make up for that when you come back we are getting along all right but we all miss you verry much and you know I do but I am so glad you are in good hands you must not come back till you are ~~good~~ well and strong if you get to lonsum let me know and I will come down and stay till you get well I will drop you a few lines every day and let you know how we are getting along we have got the house all straitened up now and it looks as well as ever Josey Maggy and I had quite a time hanging the pictures

Letter to Dear Mamie, dated August 24. (1896)

"Mamie" was Charlie's pet name for Nancy Cooper and had his friends seen one of his tender letters to her in the late summer of 1896, they wouldn't have been so skeptical that he was seriously planning marriage. They were convinced, however, when they found out that he had given her his favorite pinto horse, "Monte." As his friend Bill Rance put it, "That settles it. A man don't give a gal his hoss—not a man like Russ anyhow—'less he's plumb locoed 'bout her. He'll have to marry the gal now to git his hoss back."

in the old place

well nancy I well close for this time
with love
yns truly
C. M. Russell
Jossy and Maggy Effey Nelly
send love
we expect Mrs Roberts tomorrow
but are not sertin Mr Roberts says
he well write you tomorrow

Photograph of Charlie and Nancy with Monte.

Courtesy of F. G. Renner, Washington, D. C.

Friend Bob we recived the chickens and thank you awhollot would have written sooner but have been out of town my Father is here we have sust returned from loging creek we caught all the fish in that country I dont think

with best regards to yourself and family yours full of chicken C M Russell

Dear Mrs Thoroughman the chickens were lovley we enjoyed them so mutch it is a shame we did not wright sooner but we have been so occupied that we did not have time we have had sutch a deliteful vist with Father Russell I think he is the dearest old mann I ever saw I fell in love with him the first time I saw him we have just been travling aroun the country since he came give my love to grand ma and except a shere your self yours sincerley Mame Russell

P. S. Tell Mr Thoroughman that Father Russell did know Mr Tom Thoroughman quitte well

Letter to Bob Thoroughman, 1898

Although Charlie severed his ties with St. Louis when he was sixteen, his relations with his family remained close. During his first five years in Montana, Charlie returned annually for a few weeks with his parents. In 1898, two years after his marriage, Charlie received a visit from his father, who made the long trip to Great Falls to see his son and to welcome the new daughter-in-law to the family.

Courtesy of Robert Thoroughman, Fort Shaw, Montana

Letter to Friend Bob Thoroughman, 1899.

Keeping the wolf from the door was a struggle in the early days of the Russell marriage and a gift of chickens was a welcome addition to the larder. Charlie frequently drew only his own likeness on his letters, but here, both he and Nancy are saying "thank you" to their friend, Bob Thoroughman.

Courtesy of Robert Thoroughman, Fort Shaw, Montana

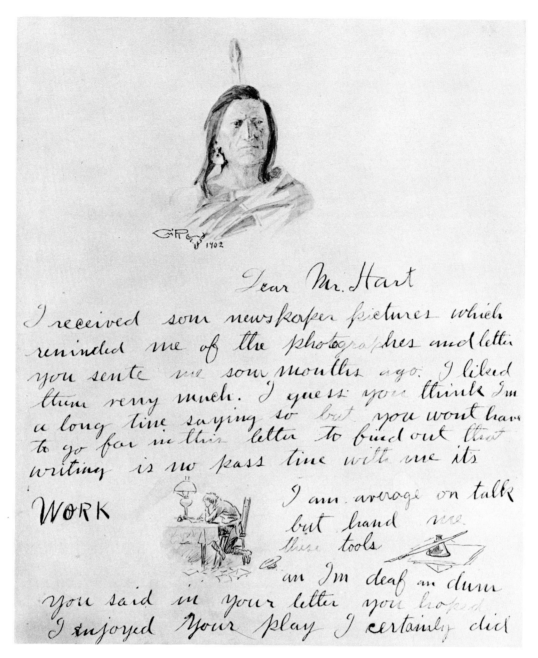

Letter to "Dear Mr. Hart" June 29, 1902

The friendship between William S. Hart and Charles M. Russell dated back to February, 1902, when Hart and a number of other actors spent the afternoon swapping yarns with Russell and some of his friends in the Park Hotel in Great Falls. That evening, Hart played the part of John Storm in "The Christian" at the Great Falls Opera House. During the performance Russell nudged his wife and said, "That feller that didn't have nothin' to say this afternoon does all the talkin' at night."

Photograph of William S. Hart and Russell

(opposite page)

William S. Hart was on the legitimate stage when he first met Russell in 1902. Twenty years later he was the foremost player of western parts on the screen, and this photograph was taken by a movie cameraman when Russell visited him "on location." After his death, Hart's home and fine collection of Russell paintings and bronzes were willed to the County of Los Angeles and is now a public park.

I have your photo hangin in my
little parler an old cow puncher friend
droped in the other day an was laking
ot the pictures an when he run on to
your photo he asked
whos the Sky pilot

well if you ever drift   west again
which I hope you will   an sight
the smoke   of my camp

Come and as our red brothers say
my pipe will be lit for you

June 27
1902

Yours Sincerly
CM Russell

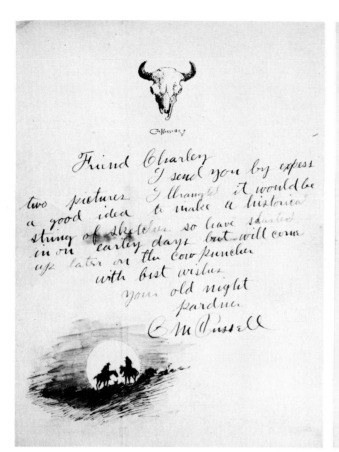
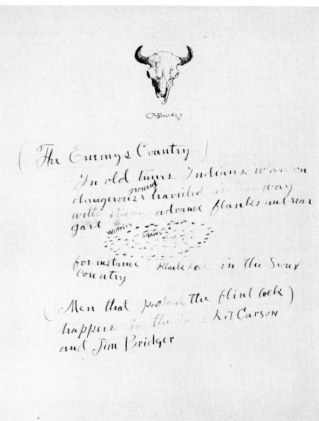

Letter to Friend Charley (Joys) undated.

The history of the American West had always been a fascinating subject to Russell and a considerable number of his paintings and drawings depicted the exploits of such explorers as Radisson, La Verendrye, Lewis and Clark, and the mountain men, Jim Bridger, Hugh Glass, and John Coulter.

The "historical string of sketches" mentioned in his letter to his old friend Charley Joys was a special set of pen and ink drawings intended for illustrations. These were completed, but were not published until after Russell's death.

The silhouette of the two mounted cowboys on the accompanying letter is unusual. Only a few such drawings by Russell are known to exist.

Courtesy of Collection of Dr. and Mrs. Franz Stenzel, Portland, Oregon

THE ENEMY'S COUNTRY. *Watercolor by Charles M. Russell*

MEN WHO PACKED THE FLINTLOCK. *Watercolor by Charles M. Russell*

Bill. Rance
Great Falls
Mont

St Louis Mo 3132 Connecticut St

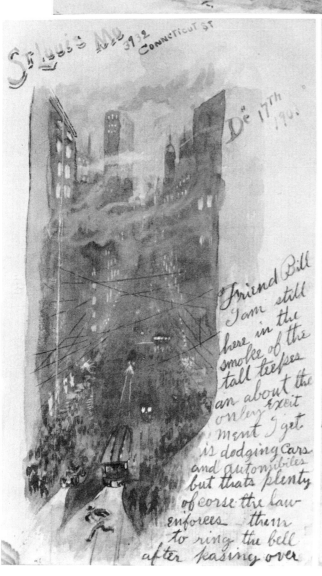

Dec 17th 1903

Friend Bill
I am still here in the smoke of the tall teepees an about the onley excit ment I get is dodging cars and automobiles but thats plenty of corse the law enforces them to ring the bell after pasing over a human but I think thats to call the wagon which hauls you to the morgue. I was out at the worlds fair ground the other day an took twenty five sents worth of automobile we hadent gon far till I'd a give more than that to walk between holding on an staying under my hat I was mighty bussy I thought the D— thing was running a way any how we were shure going sum it reminded me of some reds I had with you behind that ladys horse you used to own the one you sold in Butte he was so kind often the man is still living I have wonderd if that baught him

— 26 —

well Bill I will close
you will notice in the picture
belo I've spent money on harnes
but I'm going to dress well
if It brakes me

heres
whishing
you and all
my friends
a Merry
X Mas

Your friend
C M Russell

well be home
in about
three weeks

Letter to Bill Rance, December 17, 1903

Great Falls had few automobiles in 1903 and the opinion Russell formed when he encountered a considerable number of these new-fangled contraptions on his trip to St. Louis stayed with him all his life. He didn't like ther smell. He called them the "White Man's Skunk Wagon." He didn't like their noise. He considered the hurricane deck of a pitching bronco a far safer means of transportation.

Courtesy of the Great Falls, Montana Lodge 214
B. P. O. Elks

Photograph of St. Louis Ca. 1904-06. Courtesy of Missouri Historical Society,
St. Louis, Missouri

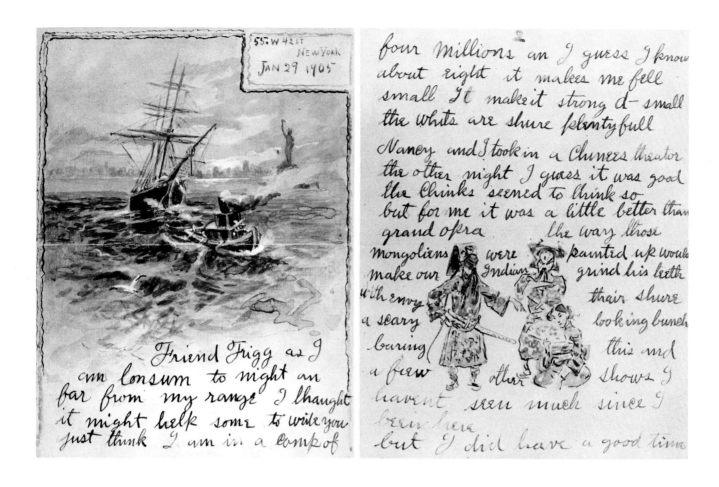

four Millions an I guess I know
about right it makes me fell
small It make it strong d= small
the Whits are shure plenty full

Nancy and I took in a Chinees theator
the other night I guess it was good
the Chinks seemed to think so
but for me it was a little better than
grand opra   the way those

Mongoliens were painted up would
make our Indian grind his teeth
with envy   thair shure
a scary   looking bunch
baring   this and
a few   other   shows I
havent   seen much since I
been here
but I did have a good time

Friend Trigg as I
am lonsum to night an
far from my range I thought
it might help some to write you
just think I am in a Comp of

Letter to "Friend Trigg," dated January 29, 1905

Albert J. Trigg was one of Russell's oldest friends and Charlie naturally turned to him when he got lonesome in New York, far from his home range. Enroute east, Charlie had stopped in St. Louis to see his father and visit the World's Fair where one of his fine paintings, "The Pirates of the Plains," had been accepted for exhibition. It was at the Fair that he saw the primitive "Iggeroties" that so fascinated him.

at the Fair the most interesting
to me were the people of the
Philipines espicially the Iggerodies
these folks are verry

primitive
there own
an
there
you

forging
weapons
weaving
own cloth but
will Notice

from this sketch that the
latter industry dos not take up much of
thair time as there wasent enough cloth
in the hole camp to up holster a cruch
they are verry small but well built people
An judging from the way they handle the spere
or assiga if they ever lern to handle
the new gun Uncle Sam is liable to
have trouble corraling em there
sirtenely a snakey looking artical
an they say they aint satisfide with
no punery suviner like a scalp

but take tha hole tok peace from
tha Adams apple up

Well Trigg how's every thing
in the Falls I havent heard
from there since I left onely
through Nancy an that dont
tell me much of the bunch
I mix with but we expect to
start home in three weeks so
Il soon know.
            with regards to
            every body in   .
                        Montana
            Your friend
                C M Russell
If you get time
    write

—29—

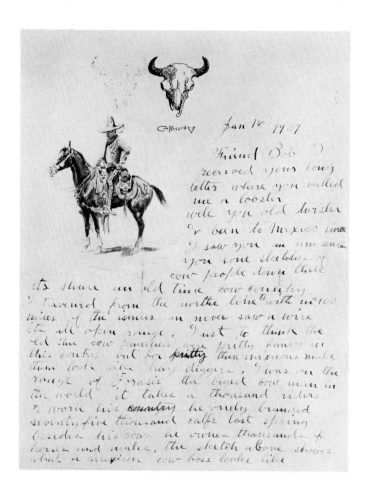

Letter to "Friend Bob" (Stuart) Jan. 10, 1907

Many an old time Montana cowboy was a fashion plate in his own right, with "horse jewelry" and fancy riggin' that cost several months' wages. Bob Stuart was one of these and Charlie knew his old friend would be interested in hearing about the appearance and equipment of the colorful vaqueros Russell had seen on his trip to Mexico.

The Amon Carter Museum, Fort Worth, Texas

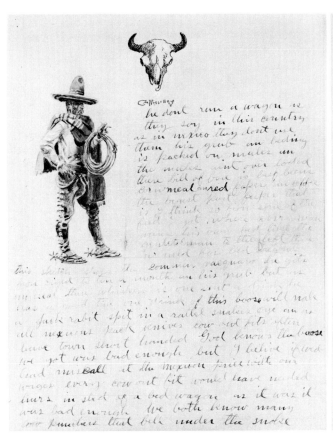

he dont run a wagon as they say in this country as in mexico they dont use them his grub an bedding is packed on mules an the mules aint over loaded thair bill of fair is beef boans cornmeal an red paper an coffe the wirst pait fair that is gitting so fare I have had gut where ever you go man his own cut finger the muleteam to the herd his meal bad has been this sketch I made the comman vaquero he gits about eight to ten a month in his pole but in mexico thair whiskey is one cent a drink he has drunk two one drink of this booze will nake a jack rabit spit in a ratel sinakes eye an as all mexicans pack knives cow out fits often leave town short handed God knows the booze we got was bad enough but I beleive if each hand mixed it the mexican prise with our wages every cow out fit would have ended theirs in sted of a bed wagon as it was it was bad enough we both know many cow punchers that bilt under the smoke

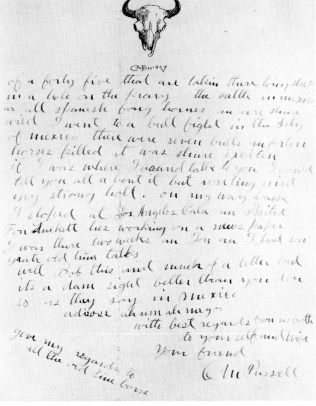

of a forty five that are takin thair long sleep in a hole on the prarie the cattle in mexico ar all spanish longy horns an are shure wild I went to a bull fight in the City of mexico thair were seven bulls an four horses killed it was shure exciten it I was where I cound talk to you I would tell you all a bout it but writing aint my strong holt on my way back I stoped at Los Angeles Cala an visited Finn Awckett hes working on a news paper I was there two weeks an Jon an I had som quite old time talks well Bob this aint much of a leter but its a dam sight better than you des so as they say in mexico adeose ahumah mego with best regards from us both give my regards to to your self and wife all the old time boys Your frend C M Russell

"MEXICAN RURALES" *Watercolor by Charles M. Russell.*

Courtesy of F. G. Renner, Washington, D. C.

Friend Trigg
I received your letter and was plenty glad to here from you

New york is as noisy as ever an baring Bronks and Central Park I dont find much to amuse me last Sunday we went to the beach an took a look at the Atlantic this little strip of water aint changed much I guess shes roling about the same as she did when old Hudson an his dutch crew sighted shore but I dont think old Henery would know the place if hed see her now. the camp s bilt up considerbul since he was here an theres more saviges

I was out at Bronks a few days ago an slayed all day they have quite a few new animals since I was here this is one of them aint he Swell

if its right that man came from monkey I savy where Baldy the bar keep got his complection of corse this is with all do respect to the monk

well Trigg as talking is easeyer for me thanwriting an I expect to see you pretty soon Ile close with best wishes to all
your friend
C M Russell

NEW YORK
NY
APR 20 1907

Letter to Friend Trigg, April 20, 1907

Charlie found New York City no more appealing in 1907 than he had on his two earlier visits. Nancy felt such trips were necessary to promote her husband's work with book publishers and art dealers, but they were not Charlie's idea of a good time. He hated the sights and sounds and smells of a big city. While he felt at home among "saviges" in Montana, they were not the same kind he met in New York.

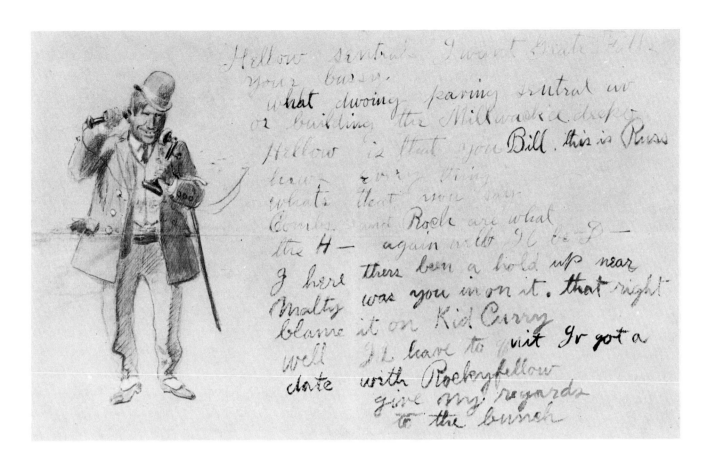

Letter to Bill Rance, April 22, 1907

"Hello Sentral"

Russell frequently illustrated his letters to his close friends with an imaginative drawing of himself. In real life, Charlie always wore his high-heeled boots and a Stetson hat, but for his friends' amusement his drawing might show him in "top hat and tails," or in a derby and spats, as in this note to Bill Rance. Rance was the owner of "The Silver Dollar Saloon" in Great Falls, and Charlie knew his letter would be shown "to the bunch" gathered there.

Me an Juck

My 3d 1907

Friend Sid for fere you will worry about me I am droping you a line. I intended leaving here several weeks ago but I cant brak away from Rockyfeller an his bunch every time I try an make a git-away he invites me up to have crackers an milk with him he shure hats to see me leave John sends his regards to the bunch an wanted me to remember him to Piano Jim an W A Clark with best wishes to friends your friend C M Russell

Letter to Friend Sid (Willis) May 3, 1907

Charlie Russell knew this account of his imaginary association with John D. "Rockyfeller" would tickle the fancy of his old cronies at "The Mint."

Coupling the name of "Piano Jim," ex-gunman, faro dealer and bouncer, who fell on evil days and became the piano-playing "professor" in a honky-tonk, with that of W. A. Clark, millionaire and ex-United States Senator from Montana, was the final touch of his puckish humor.

The Amon Carter Museum, Fort Worth, Texas

Booklet, "Piano Jim and the Impotent Pumpkin Vine"
Courtesy of F. G. Renner, Washington, D. C.

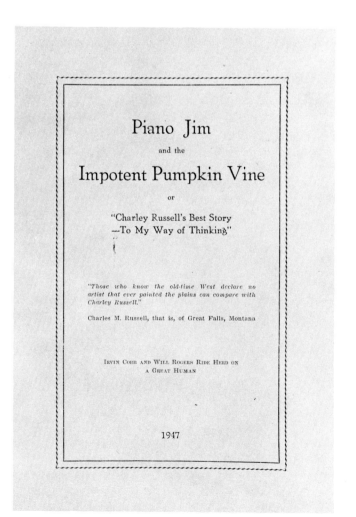

Piano Jim

and the

Impotent Pumpkin Vine

or

"Charley Russell's Best Story
—To My Way of Thinking"

"Those who know the old-time West declare no artist that ever painted the plains can compare with Charley Russell."

Charles M. Russell, that is, of Great Falls, Montana

IRVIN COBB AND WILL ROGERS RIDE HERD ON
A GREAT HUMAN

1947

Letter to Friend Ed Botsford, 1910

Russell never forgot his early range days, or the friends he made then. As a youngster, Botsford "went up the trail" from Texas, worked as a cowboy in Montana for many years, and later was a top rider for the Miller Brothers 101 Wild West Show. After leaving the show, he returned to his home in Littlefield, Texas.

The horse Russell has shown in his drawing was his favorite mount "Red Bird."

Courtesy of J. Frank Dobie, Austin, Texas

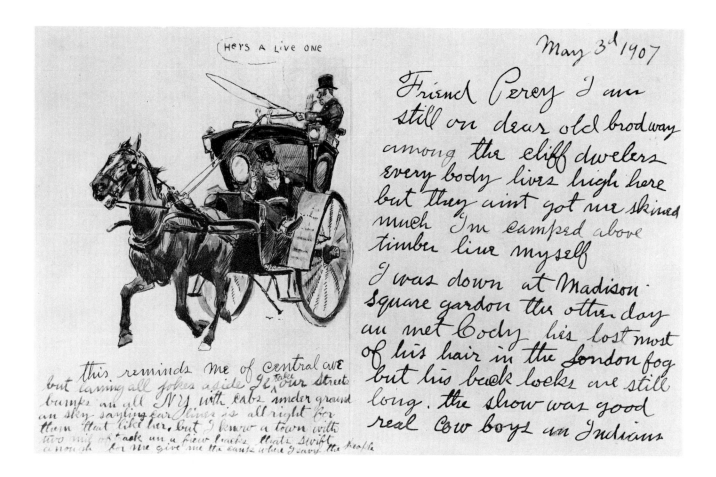

(HEYS A LIVE ONE

May 3d 1907

Friend Percy I am still on dear old brodway among the cliff dwelers every body lives high here but they aint got me skined much I'm camped above timber line myself

I was down at Madison square gardon the other day an met Cody his lost most of his hair in the London fog but his back locks are still long. the show was good real Cow boys an Indians

this reminds me of central ave but larving all jokes aside I'le take your struts bumps an all NY with cabs under ground an sky saylying car lines is all right for them that like her, but I know a town with two mil of track an a few buicks thats swift a nouch for me give me the cants where I saw the People

Letter to Friend Percy (Raban) May 3, 1907

Present-day movie and TV producers didn't start the practice of putting outandish costumes on their cowboys and Indians. They have merely made it worse. This letter suggests that Buffalo Bill Cody was one of the first showmen to put red shirts on his cowboys and sleigh bells on Indians.

Courtesy of the William E. Weiss, Jr., Collection, Whitney Gallery of Western Art, Cody, Wyoming.

Modern-day historians discredit many of the exploits attributed to William F. Cody during his army scouting days but there is no question that, as a showman, he did more than any other individual to establish the image of the Wild West in the popular mind. "Buffalo Bill's Wild West and Congress of Rough Riders of the World" appealed to young and old, in this country and abroad, and even Charlie Russell thought it was "all right" when he saw the show in New York City in 1907.

Photograph of Buffalo Bill, Courtesy of the Historical Society of Montana, Helena, Montana.

Ronan
Flathead
Resirvation
1908

Friend Thed Com on an bring
the bunch the lids off up here
there playing on the first floor
black jack an monty wide open
be carful an dont tip it off to non
of them morilests
                    with regards to the bunch
                         your frend
                              C M Russell

Letter to Friend Thed (Gibson) 1908

All of the Plains Indian tribes loved to gamble and it didn't take them long to adopt some of the white man's games, particularly poker and "monty." After the Indians were placed on reservations their gambling was frowned on by officials, but little could be done about it. Charlie's friend Thed (Theodore Gibson) and his brother Phil owned the Park Hotel in Great Falls where gambling was an accepted social custom. Coming from a family of early frontiersmen, the Gibson brothers were not numbered among the moralists mentioned in the letter.

Letter to Mr. Douglas, January 12, 1910.

In 1908, the Canadian government bought part of the famous Pablo Buffalo herd on the Flathead Indian Reservation in Montana, at the time the largest herd of these animals in existence. After two weeks of hard riding the picked crew of seventy-five Montana cowboys managed to corral only 120 of the animals. The buffalo repeatedly charged the cowboys, broke the barriers erected to control them, and stampeded over cliffs to escape. Russell was along as guest of the Canadian officials, and as a result of this experience left a record in oil and watercolor of a number of stirring incidents of the drive. This is the buffalo round-up mentioned in the accompanying letter to Mr. Douglas.

an the doclers found out I had
the price so called it appendeeitis
I think that the way its spelt
aney how she got the knife an
were both trimed now. as you
know I got mine two years
ago
if a man gets a belly ake these days
he wants to cash his role an play
broke My wife was pritty sick for
a while but she is getting along
fine now
I got a lot of pictures from Hammoud
and Mactavish they were fine I
am having a book made of them
it will be good to look at in years
to com
I will never forget that buffalo
round up an will always be
thank ful to you for the good time
I had whishing you a happy
new year I am your friend
C M Russell

THE LAST
of the
BUFFALO

Comprising a history
of the Buffalo herd at the
Flathead reservation and
an account of the last great
Buffalo roundup.

Charles M. Russell as a participant in the
"Pablo Buffalo Round-up", October 1908.
The river in the background is the Pend
d'Oreille.

Photograph of Russell on Buffalo Round-up:
Courtesy of F. G. Renner, Washington, D. C.

Booklet, "The Last of the Buffalo."
Courtesy of F. G. Renner, Washington, D.C.

Piegan Blackfeet in Glacier Park from Photo
by Rolland Reed.

Jim Gabreil and band of Sioux
Buffalo Bill Show — about 1904

As a youngster, Jim Gabril rode for the Francis E. Warren outfit on Cow Creek in Wyoming. In 1890 he left the ranch to serve as a dispatch rider for General Miles. Later he turned to show business and was a bronc rider with Buffalo Bill for ten years. During the World's Fair in St. Louis in 1904 he had his own wild west show at the Delmar Gardens, St. Louis. It is probable that this is where he and Charlie Russell first met. The Gabril Wild West Show later performed in Liverpool and Manchester, England, and in 1909 was one of the featured attractions at the Alaska-Yukon-Pacific Exposition in Seattle, Washington.

Photograph of Jim Gabril with Indians from the Buffalo Bill Show: Courtesy the Log Cabin Studio, Great Falls, Montana

Courtesy of the C. M. Russell Gallery, Great Falls, Montana

Letter to Jim Gabril, 1910

Jim Gabril, who is shown with Charlie Russell in the accompanying letter, was one of the leading bronco busters of his time. It is probable that Charlie saw him perform on numerous occasions. They were the same age and, in their earlier days, had shared the same experiences. One was to become famous as a bronc rider and the other as the "Cowboy Artist." Russell's comment in the verse accompanying his drawings, that "he aint pulled leather yet" was the highest tribute he could have paid to his friend's ability as a "bronc twister."

Courtesy of John S. du Mont, O. S. J., Greenfield, Massachusetts

To Jim. Gabril
From his friend
C. M. Russell

1910

Hang an rattel Jimmy
com back an get your gun
the wether must be warme up there
your mighty near the sun

That hoss is shure a wearing fin
but your still on his hump
if you had annother arme ar two
youd qurt him every jump

No Jinny aint no frade strap man
he aint pulled leather yet
well he ride him, well I'd tell a man
its the safest kind o bet
The playfull way hes cashed his head
shows plane hes after you
scratch him on the sholder fin
hes playing peek a boo

Hell o Trigg I'm here
in the big Canak
an have visited all the places that
interest me. an am getting lonsum
for home
I was down to the aquarium
the other day they have quite
a number of new fish
I walked back through Bowling
Green which I belive is the oldest
part of the burg
this is where the Dutch uste to
play ten pins

Hello Trigg, April 10, 1911

Albert Trigg's people had come from England, a land Russell called a "cold bread country." Like many an Englishman, Trigg was interested in history and Russell delighted in illustrating his letters with characters from its pages. These ranged from pirates of the Spanish Main to iron-hatted soldiers of Cromwell's time. Here Russell has shown some of the pantalooned burghers of early-day New York trading with the Indians before "Mose Kaufman's cousins" acquired a "large interist in the city."

Courtesy of the C. M. Russell Gallery, Great Falls, Montana

an trade with the Indians.
I think it was these limburger
eaters that told the red man
to plant powder an ball
Mr Ingen put in this crop the
sam as corn.
but not beeing a up to date scien
tific dry lander his crop failed.
the dutch like all good boosters
looked sorry an told him he hadent
harrowed it under properly
that by plowing deep an roling
the soil would hold moister that
it never had. the same as it did
for our farmer last summer.
did this stop the red man this
plum failure of powder an ball crop
No He started raising Hair with
out errigation this crop
was shurer but had its
draw backs imagin
a savig who lived in the swet
sucking woods rasing the
hair of a dutch man with
limburger in every pocket
it must have ban tough.
right heres Trigg
I got hazy on history
of this Island but the Injun

quit it and the English got
it away from the Dutch.
I dont know who owns it now
but as every other man looks
like Mose Kaufmans cousin
I think Jerusilam has a large
interest here
we took in a Sufferegte
marting the other night an
a finer band of Hellraisers
I never saw bunched
according to there argument
men would have littel to say
in regards to goverment
I will tell you all a bout it
when I see you
but will close for this time
with regards to all
Your friend
C M Russell
Apral 10
1911

Albert J. Trigg, from a portrait by William Krieghoff. Courtesy of the C. M.
Russell Gallery, Great Falls, Montana

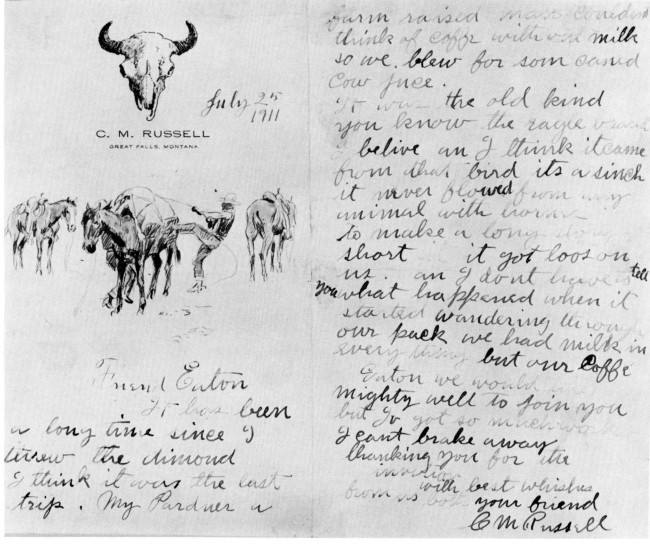

Letter to Friend Eaton, July 25, 1911

How to keep an opened can of milk from leaking was always a problem with the old timers traveling by pack train. One way was to seal the two holes with a thumbnail-sized piece of paper, hoping the stickiness of the milk would hold them in place. Another was to plug the holes with a sharpened twig. Apparently neither of these methods worked for Charlie.

Courtesy of Mrs. William Eaton, Wolf, Wyoming

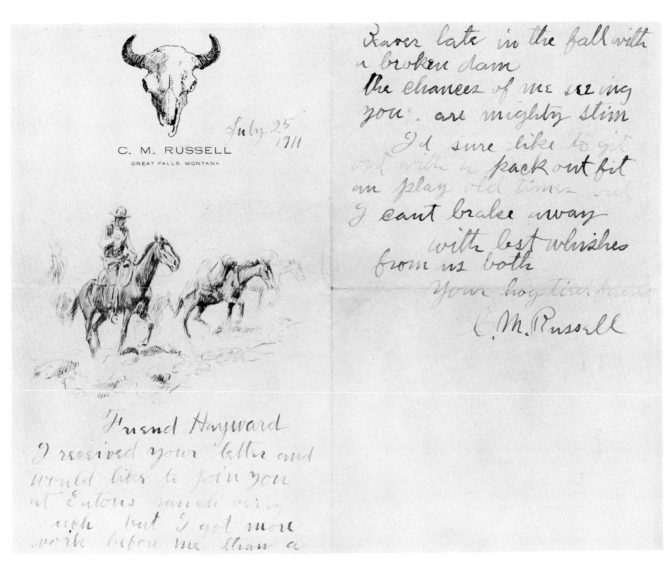

Letter to Friend Hayward, July 25, 1911.

It is small wonder that Russell had to decline the invitation from Harry Hayward to visit the dude ranch of their mutual friend, Howard Eaton, at Wolf, Wyoming. In 1911 Russell had his first major exhibition in New York City, completed eighty-six illustrations for the book *Fifteen Thousand Miles by Stage,* and in July was still faced with a commission for another forty-odd drawings for the special edition of Owen Wister's *The Virginian.* Between times, there were four important oil paintings to finish. There is no question that he had more work "than a beaver late in the fall with a broken dam."

Courtesy of Marion W. Niedringhaus, Ladue, Missouri

Russell's friend, Howard Eaton, originally an easterner from Pittsburg, headed west in 1879 to the Badlands of North Dakota where he was a ranching neighbor of Theodore Roosevelt. He moved on to Wolf Creek, Wyoming, in 1904, to establish one of the first, and most famous cow and dude ranches, Eaton's Ranch. In 1915, Eaton took the Russells on a pack trip into some of the most spectacular back-country of western Montana. Mary Roberts Rinehart was also a member of the party and the trip is described in rich detail in her book, *Through Glacier National Park—Seeing America First with Howard Eaton.*

Photograph of Howard Eaton, Dude Rancher.

Courtesy of the Log Cabin Studio, Great Falls, Montana

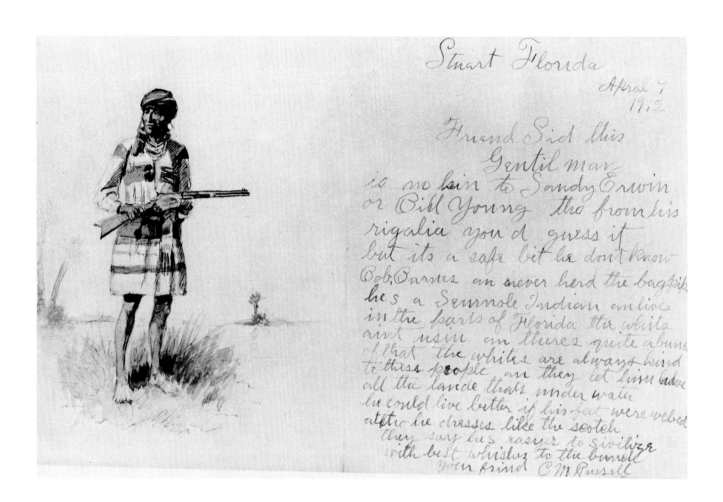

Letter to Friend Sid, April 7, 1912.

Only Russell would have seen the resemblance between the skirt of a Seminole Indian in Florida and the kilts of his Scottish friends back in Great Falls. Sandy Erwin was the Great Falls blacksmith who shod Charlie's saddle horses and Bill Young was their mutual friend. Young was better known as "Bull Trout," for his inclination to spend most of his time fishing.

The Amon Carter Museum, Fort Worth, Texas

Photograph of Trigg and Russell in Camp

Albert Trigg met Charles M. Russell in Great Falls in the winter of 1891 and from that day the two men were fast friends. Trigg encouraged the young artist and was, in fact, one of the first to help sell some of his paintings. Years later Charlie told about a sales talk Trigg had given a visiting wool buyer who had indicated an interest in buying two paintings. Trigg passed the word on, and in a few days Charlie completed two watercolors and brought them around. As Charlie told it, "He seemed real pleased and asks, 'How much?' Now this feller's a plumb stranger so I figgers I'll hit him hard and sez 'Fifty dollars.' An' I'm a common liar if that feller don't dig out a hundred dollars and hand em over. He thinks I mean fifty dollars a piece and don't know to this day how bad he beat himself."

Courtesy of the Historical Society of Montana, Helena, Montana

Letter to Friend Trigg, April 7, 1912

When Russell visited strange places, his artist's eye invariably peopled the country with the colorful characters who had once lived there. These frequently appeared in beautifully executed little watercolors on his letters.

Courtesy of the C. M. Russell Gallery, Great Falls, Montana

Letter to Bill Rance, August 12, 1912

Knowing that the Russells were convivial hosts at their summer lodge on Lake McDonald in Glacier National Park, Charlie's friends frequently sent appropriate gifts. The cigars Charlie is handing out in the sketch on the accompanying letter were probably the "Charles M. Russell" brand that his friend Bill Rance had specially packed for sale at his "Silver Dollar" saloon in Great Falls.

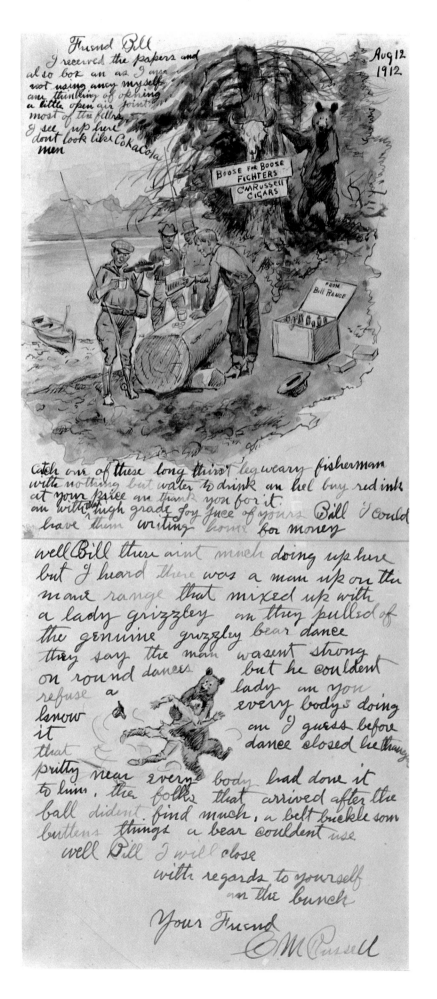

As his reputation as "the Cowboy Artist" became established, Russell's name, as well as his pictures, was used in a number of astonishing ways. Today Russell enthusiasts collect such little known items as phony money, World War I posters, and silk fans with examples of Charlie's art on them. Among the most sought-after of Russell ephemera is the C. M. Russell cigar box, that once held "a good five-cent cigar."

Letter to Friend Guy, October 13, 1912

In the spring of 1912 a young Wyoming cowboy named Guy Weadick arrived in Calgary, Alberta with a dream. This was to promote a contest that would pit the State champions of the United States and Mexico against the best riders and ropers that Canada could produce, then top it off with the greatest assemblage of Plains Indians the world had ever seen. With Weadick's contagious enthusiasm, $20,-000 in gold was raised for prize money and the first Calgary Stampede was born. The show was quickly recognized as one of the West's greatest rodeos.

Never one to waste words, Russell gave, in this long letter to his friend Weadick, a high tribute to the riding and roping he saw at this first Stampede.

The Amon Carter Museum, Fort Worth, Texas

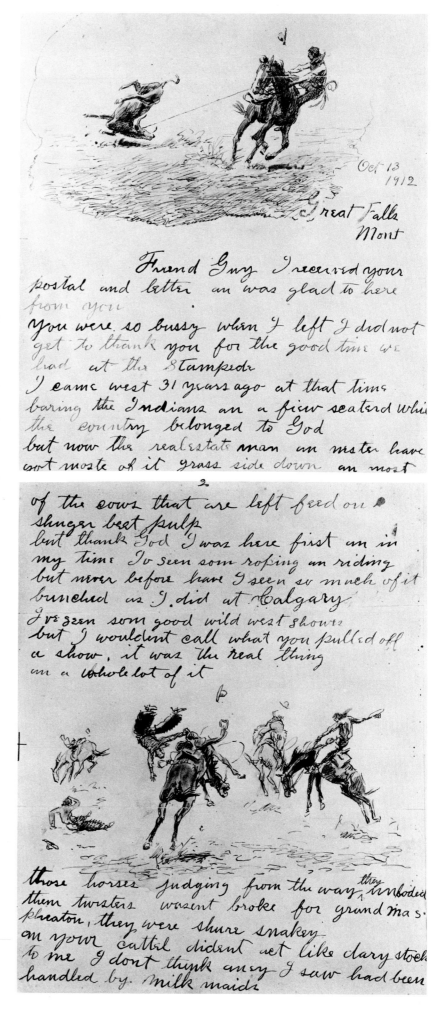

Oct 13
1912
Great Falls
Mont

Friend Guy I received your
postal and letter an was glad to here
from you
You were so bussy when I left I did not
get to thank you for the good time we
had at the Stampede
I came west 31 years ago at that time
baring the Indians an a fiew seaterd whit
the country belonged to God
but now the realestate man an mister have
cut moste of it grass side down an most

of the sows that are left feed on
slinger beet pulp
but thank God I was here first an in
my time Iv seen som roping an riding
but never before have I seen so much of it
bunched as I did at Calgary
Ive seen som good wild west shows
but I wouldent call what you pulled off
a show, it was the real thing
an a whole lot of it

those horses judging from the way they unbodec
them twisters wasent broke for grand ma s
pheaton, they were shure snakey
an your cattel dident act like dary stock
to me I dont think enny I saw had been
handled by milk maids

they were shure a surprise to those old cow poneys that had been running short horns all there life. It wasent hardly fair to spring a gray hound wareing horns

an Guy foot ball aint so gentel—the
bull ring an prise fighting is som rough
but bull doging those long horns makes
all other dangirous sports look lik
nursery games
I am not alone   in my
krause of the   Stampede
there are other   men
better judges
                              than myself.
Make the same talk
            With best whishes from
                my wift and I
                    to you and yours
        your friend C M Russell

Photograph of Guy Weadick. Courtesy of Fred
Kennedy, Calgary, Alberta, Canada

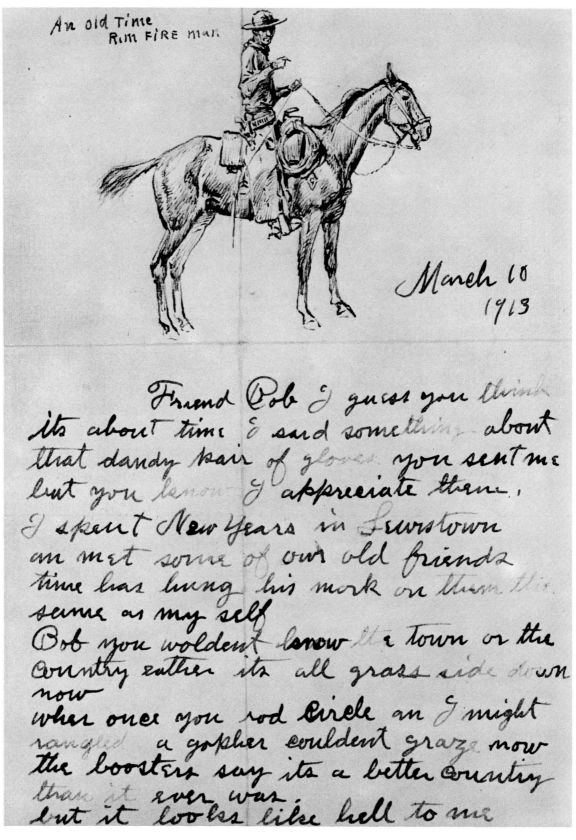

An old Time
Rim Fire man

March 10
1913

Friend Bob I guess you think
its about time I said something about
that dandy pair of gloves you sent me
but you know I appreciate them,
I spent New Years in Lewistown
an met some of our old friends
time has hung his mark on them the
same as my self
Bob you woldent know the town or the
Country eather its all grass side down
now
wher once you rod circle an I might
rangled a gopher couldent graze now
the boosters say its a better country
than it ever was.
but it looks like hell to me

Letter to Friend Bob, March 10, 1913.

Like most other early-day cowboys, Charlie's friend Bob Stuart was "an old-time rim-fire man," using a single cinch on his saddle instead of the double-rig outfit that came up the trail from Texas. When Charlie and Bob wintered together in Lewistown after the fall round-up of 1890, this entire area was open range. Twenty-three years later Charlie was saddened to find much of this wonderful country that had "belonged to God" has been turned "grass side down" and now looked like hell.

The Amon Carter Museum, Fort Worth, Texas

I liked it better twen it belonged to God
It was shure lind country when we knew it
    Bob I wish you had been at
Calgary last fall they pulled off
som good riding and roping thare

but thare was quite a fiw rode like
the above sketch
I ust to ride that way myself in old
days I think it was called riding with
a role
of corse there was lots of good rids
made but I'd like to see one of these
up to date twisters ride one of those
old time low cantil flat horn shells
cow punchers ust to ride
I think it would bother them sum
well Bob Il close.
            with best whishes
                to your self and Wife
        from us both
            your friend
                C M Russell
regards
to all friends

THE NEWCOME
PORT SEWALL, FLORIDA

March 30
1913

Friend Trigg
        I do not blame old
Ponce de Leon for thinking He
had hit an inchantid land
which held a spring that would

Letter to Friend Trigg, March 30, 1913.

The Russell's first trip to Florida was in 1912. Charlie was so fascinated with the country that he and Nancy returned again the following year. Charlie found the warm sunshine a pleasant relief from the Montana winter and he called Florida "a good lay-around country."

Courtesy of the C. M. Russell Gallery, Great Falls, Montana

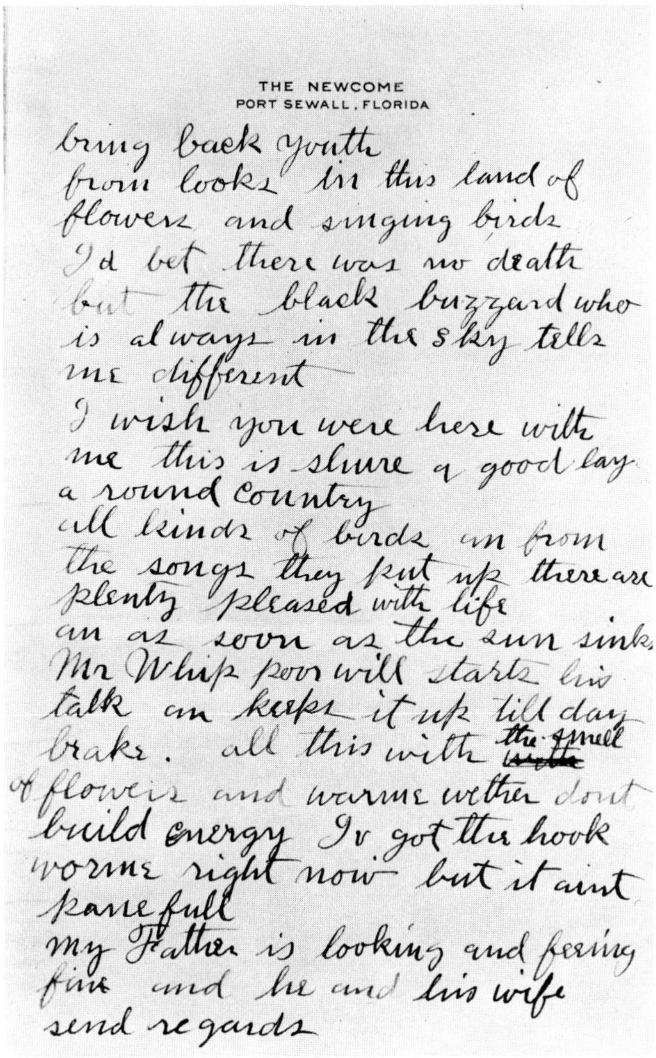

bring back youth
from looks in this land of
flowers and singing birds
I'd bet there was no death
but the black buzzard who
is always in the sky tells
me different
I wish you were here with
me this is shure a good lay
a round country
all kinds of birds an from
the songs they put up there are
plenty pleased with life
an as soon as the sun sinks
Mr Whip poor will starts his
talk an keeps it up till day
brake. all this with the smell
of flowers and warme wether dont
build energy Iv got the hook
worme right now but it aint
pane full
my Father is looking and feeling
fine and he and his wife
send regards

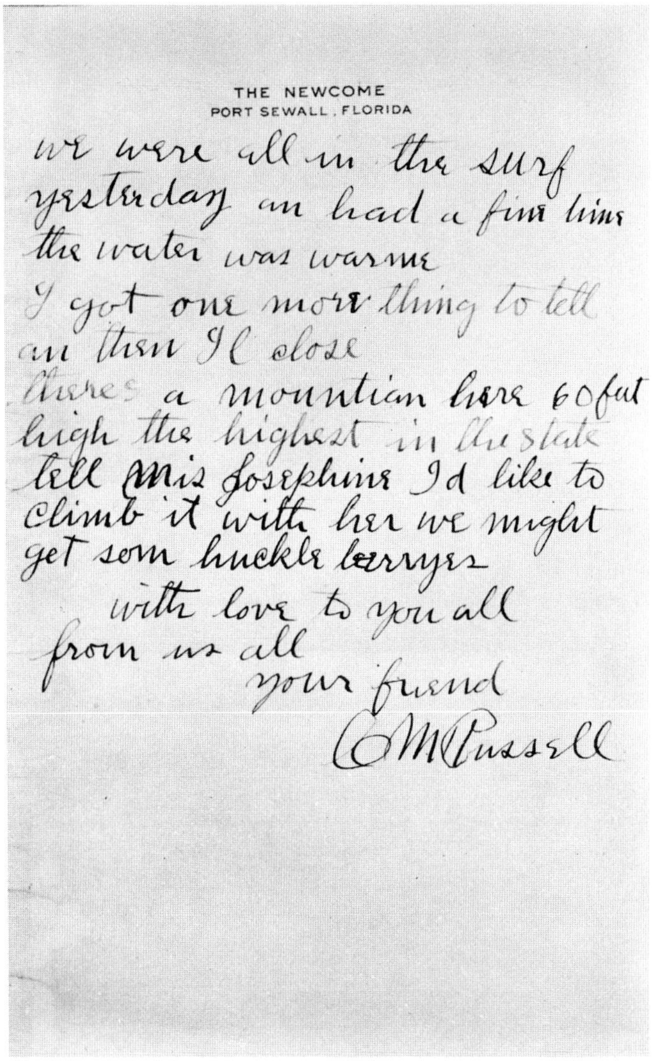

we were all in the surf
yesterday an had a fine time
the water was warme
I got one more thing to tell
an then Il close
theres a mountian here 60 fut
high the highest in the state
tell Mis Josephine I'd like to
climb it with her we might
get som huckle berryes
    with love to you all
from us all
        your friend
        CMRussell

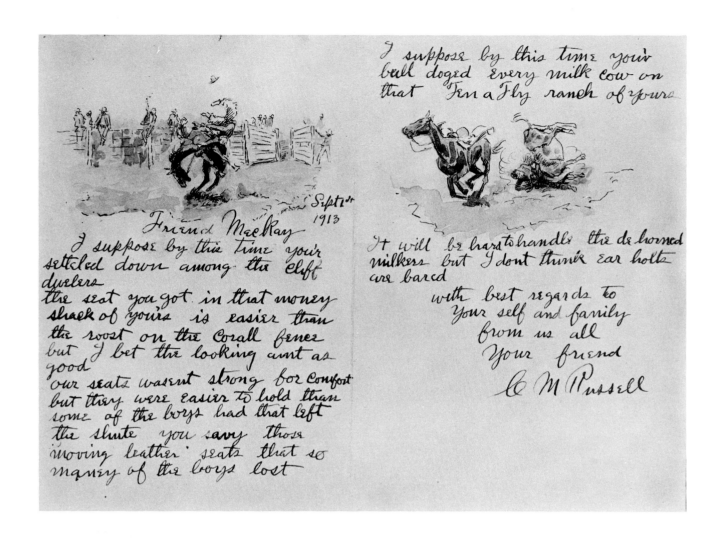

Letter to Friend Mackay, September 1, 1913.

After his years in the West, Russell's friend Malcolm Mackay returned to the skyscrapers of New York to re-enter the banking business, commuting to his offices from the family home at Tenafly, New Jersey. Russell's letter gently reminded his old friend not to forget his experiences as a Montana rancher.

Courtesy of the Malcolm S. Mackay Family

April 20 1914

Friend Percy

here I am in Old **London** an it's sure antique

I was up north of the big camp the other day where stands an old monistary all so a wall built by the romans built I suppose to protect them from Dinny Doolins forefathers who crosed the chanel once an a while in there bull boats headed with clubs of black thorne an stone axes to prove to the gladitors that life wasent no lengethy pickinic

I was told that this country was also the home range of William the Conqueror a gentle man whos history would make Sitting Bull look like Brother Van

I found a pack of woods that was realy lonsum an I couldent helpe but wonder what would happen . if the wheel of time would slide her cogs an slide back to the tenth sentury like Mark Twains yankie

A fine chance I'd a stood in this timber afoot if Bill Conk an his bunch of killers had of rode on to me dressed in their steel chain union suits their'd been nothing for me but take my hat off an make a squaring talk or sing God save the King

Well Percy I will have to close as we are going out in the country with best wishes from us both to you and yors

Your friend
CM Russell

Address Dore Gallery
35 New Bond St
London

Letter to Friend Percy Raban, April 20, 1914.

Although Charlie took the time to visit a number of places in England while his paintings were being shown at the Dore Galleries in London, he did not forget to write home.

In mentioning "Dinny Doolin's forefathers" in his letter to Percy Raban, Russell was undoubtedly thinking of their mutual Irish friend, D. C. Dulin, the first proprietor of "The Mint" saloon in Great Falls. "Brother Van" was, of course, the popular Methodist missionary Russell had first met in Pigeye Basin on the headwaters of the Judith River in the early '80's.

Photograph of Brother Van.

"Brother Van" (William Wesley Van Orsdel) who is mentioned in the accompanying letter, arrived in Montana in the summer of 1872 as a young Methodist missionary, having paid for his passage up the Missouri River by singing to his fellow passengers. Russell and Brother Van met some years later when the two of them happened to stop for the night with a character called "Old Bab" who had a cabin in Pigeye Basin. Observant as always, Russell noted that although the stranger was in frontier garb, his hands were not those of a mountain man. His blurted remark that "You're either a preacher or a tin-horn gambler" was the start of their life-long friendship.

Letter to Friend Ben (Stephens) undated.

As this letter suggests, Russell's early friends had only to ask for one or more of his paintings and in due time they would be delivered. The ones that "didn't turn out good" were probably tossed in the fire.

Ben Stephens and Charlie Russell arrived in Montana the same year (1880) but didn't become friends until they met five years later when they were both working for the Choteau Livestock Company. Stephens later located his own ranch near Dodson in the Judith Basin where Charlie was a frequent visitor.

Courtesy of John S. du Mont, O. S. J., Greenfield, Massachusetts

Letter to Friend Sid, April 20, 1914.

As an artist, Russell was undoubtedly fascinated with the colorful trappings of royalty and many of the letters he sent back from England were illustrated with delightful little watercolors of real or imaginary royal guards, court jesters, and armored knights. Most of the letters reveal his deep feeling that this was not his country nor these his people, and his homesickness for friends in Montana. As he once remarked, "Altho I'm glad I went I did not shed maney tears leaving the home of my ansesters."

The Amon Carter Museum, Fort Worth, Texas

The occasion for this letter to Sid Willis, was a momentous one: Charlie's trip to England for his first showing abroad at the famous Dore Gallery, 35 New Bond Street, London. Outdoor action pictures appealed to the English and the exhibition of twenty-five of Russell's larger oils and watercolors, named "The West that has Passed," received favorable notice in the London press. A number of the paintings were sold to English purchasers, although after the First World War some found their way back to the United States.

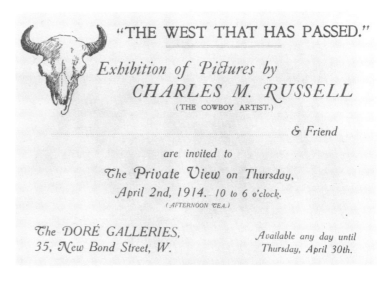

"THE WEST THAT HAS PASSED."

Exhibition of Pictures by
CHARLES M. RUSSELL
(THE COWBOY ARTIST.)

& Friend

are invited to
The *Private View* on Thursday,
April 2nd, 1914. 10 to 6 o'clock.
(AFTERNOON TEA.)

The DORÉ GALLERIES,
35, New Bond Street, W.

Available any day until
Thursday, April 30th.

Invitation to Dore Gallery Exhibition. Courtesy of F. G. Renner, Washington, D. C.

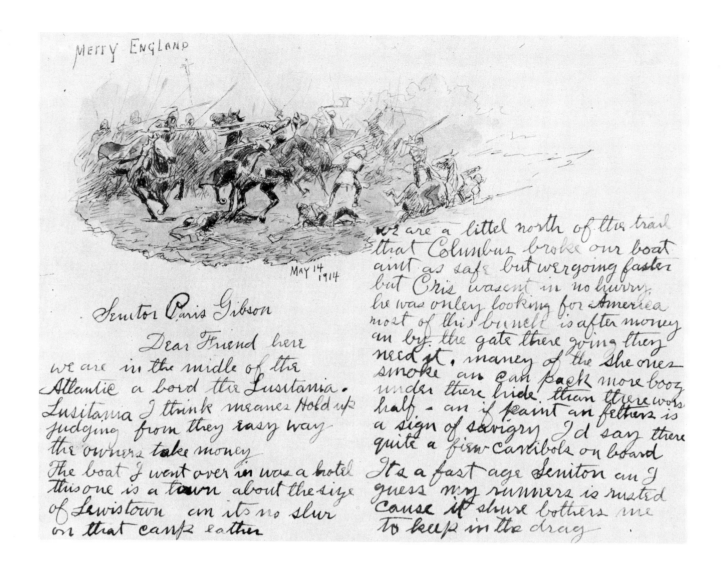

MERRY ENGLAND

MAY 14 1914

Senitor Paris Gibson

Dear Friend here
we are in the midle of the
Atlantic a bord the Lusitania.
Lusitania I think meanes Hold up
judging from they easy way
the owners take money
The boat I went over in was a hotel
this one is a town about the size
of Lewistown an its no slur
on that camp eather

we are a littel north of the trail
that Columbus broke our boat
aint as safe but wergoing faster
but Cris wasent in no hurry.
he was onley looking for America
most of this bunch is after money
an by the gate there going they
need it. maney of the she ones
smoke an can pack more booz
under there hide than there wors
half — an if paint an fethers is
a sign of savigry I'd say there
quite a fiew canibols on board
Its a fast age Seniton an I
guess my runners is rusted
cause it shure bothers me
to keep in the drag

Letter to Paris Gibson, May 14, 1914.

Charlie's return from his first trip abroad was on the great Cunard liner, "The Lusitania," fated to be torpedoed off the coast of Ireland just a year later (May 7, 1915.) His interesting comments about his fellow passengers apparently shocked eastern editors when they saw this letter some years later. In any event, when the letter was published in the book, *Good Medicine,* they deleted the part that mentioned "maney of the she ones smoke an can pack more booz under there hide than there worst half—an if paint an fethers is a sign of savigry, I'd say there quite a fiew canibols on board."

Courtesy of F. G. Renner, Washington, D. C.

I have seen quite a little of old England an its sertenly a pritty country like one great park. with an interesting history I riseted seviral hang outs of Bill the Conquar saw walls and rodes built before Bill landed by the Romans. saw the ax and block where many politicans lost there office. an when I looked at that old rustay ax I couldent help thinking that it might be a good thing these days It sertanly has made a clean quiet country of England a land which for centuries lay seeped in blood the history of our country has quite a littel read in it but its pale compared to this land our Injun was a ware lover but blamed no God for the blood he spilt neather for cross or king did he war but for his country an well we know it was worth fighting for a Dam good country an a Dam good cause the Injun was bad all right but Senator if time were to slip her cogs an drop back some senturies I'd prefur seary America to Merry England well Senator as I know I can talk better at close range Il quit firing at long

with best whishes
to You and most of the
folks in Montana
Your friend
C M Russell

Paris Gibson, one of Montana's distinguished citizens, was 83 years of age when he received this letter from Charlie Russell. Paris Gibson first saw the upper falls of the Missouri in May, 1882. Impressed with the area's great natural resources, he enlisted the financial backing of James J. Hill and proceeded to lay out the broad streets and public parks that was to become the city of Great Falls. After serving as the first mayor of the town, Paris Gibson helped to draw up the first constitution for the State of Montana and in 1901 was elected to the United States Senate.

Years later, Charlie was to pay a tribute to his friend's vision. Recalling that he had once night herded on the spot where the town was built and that others considered it good beef country, he remarked that "it remained for the eyes of his friend he called "Camp Finder" to see a great city where there was only prairie and rivers."

Photograph of Paris Gibson.

Courtesy of the Great Falls Tribune, Great Falls, Montana

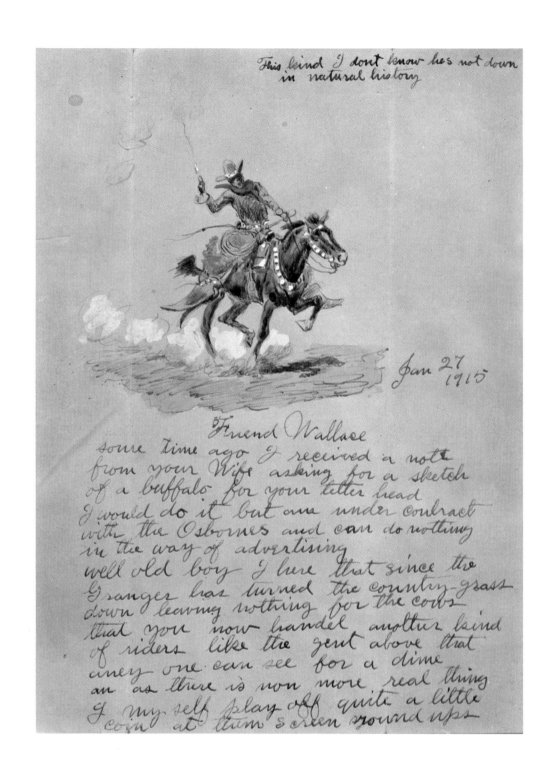

This kind I dont know hes not down in natural history

Jan 27 1915

Friend Wallace

soure time ago I received a note from your Wife asking for a sketch of a buffalo for your letter head I would do it but am under contract with the Osbornes and can do nothing in the way of advertising

well old boy I here that since the Granger has turned the country-grass down leaving nothing for the cows that you now handel another kind of riders like the gent above that aney one can see for a dime an as there is non more real thing I my self play off quite a little coin at them screen round ups

Letter to Friend Wallace Coburn, Jan. 27, 1915.

When Charlie Russell made the little ink and watercolor sketch of "an old-time cow dog" and reminded his friend that "we both knew this kind," he was no doubt thinking of their days together twenty-five years earlier on the old Circle C. Ranch on Beaver Creek in Montana. The movie cowboy depicted in the other sketch is still with us, but it has been a long time since he "can be seen for a dime," as Charlie pointed out in 1915.

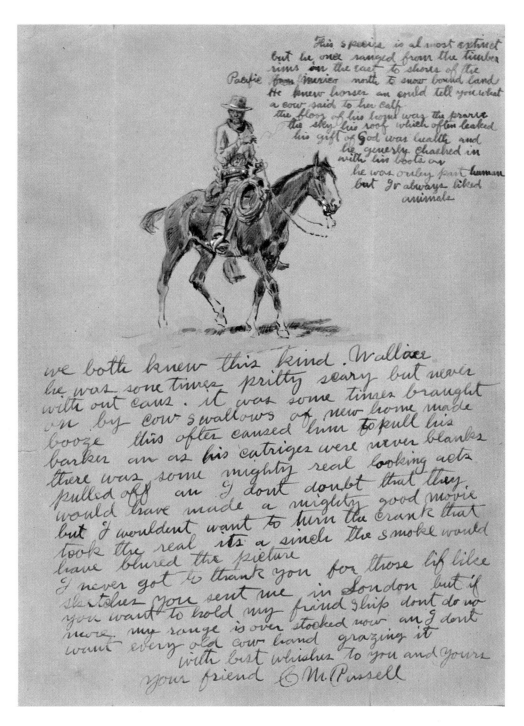

This species is almost extinct but he once ranged from the timber rims on the east to shores of the Pacific from Mexico north to snow bound land He knew horses an could tell you what a cow said to her calf the floor of his home was the prarie the sky his roof which often leaked his gift of God was health and he generly cashed in with his boots on he was onley part human but I always liked animals

we both knew this kind. Wallace he was some times pritty scary but never with out caus. it was some times braught on by cow swallows of new home made booze this ofter caused him to pull his barker an as his catriges were never blanks there was some mighty real looking acts pulled off an I dont doubt that they would have made a mighty good movie but I wouldent want to turn the crank that took the real its a sinch the smoke would have blured the picture I never got to thank you for those lif like sketches you sent me in London but if you want to hold my friend ship dont do no more. my range is over stocked now an I dont want every old cow hand grazing it with best wishes to you and yours your friend C M Russell

Columbia Pictures photograph of Wallace Coburn by Bob Coburn

Courtesy of Mrs. Wallace D. Coburn, Santa Barbara, California

Wallace David Coburn was another of Charlie Russell's friends who became associated with the arts. Coburn grew up in the Chestnut Valley near White Sulphur Springs and later was a partner with his father in the Coburn Cattle Company, a 25,000-head outfit that ranged over much of Central Montana. Charlie Russell wrangled horses for this outfit in 1890 and their Circle C, CK, Wineglass, Bar L and Rafter T brands appear in many of his paintings. In 1899, Coburn published a little book of western verse, *Rhymes From a Round-Up Camp* which was illustrated by Russell. Since Russell was already known as "The Cowboy Artist," Coburn's book led to his appellation as "The Cowboy Poet." Like many another old-time cowboy, Coburn later went to Hollywood where he appeared in numerous movies with Bill Hart, Hoot Gibson, and Tom Mix. Eventually he formed his own firm, The Great Western Film Company.

Letter to Friend Kilroy, undated.

Richard R. Kilroy, famous newspaperman who was to become the financial editor of the San Francisco Chronicle, never forgot his early days in Montana in the '90's when he and Charlie Russell were night-herding together for the old Circle C Ranch on the slopes of the Little Rockies.

Thirty years later Charlie was to write, "Friend Dick: You need no book to help you remember the west you knew and loved. She was a sweetheart of yours and mine, a wild maid with maney lovers. She knew little of law but used no keys and aney body's money was safer in a little wooden box guarded by only a booz soaked bartender than it is today behind steel and time locks. The West we knew, Dick, is an old woman now but we still love her. The reformers will bury her without flowers but her name will live in the harts of her lovers and history when the names of those who screwed down the lid are long forgotten. Your friend, C. M. Russell."

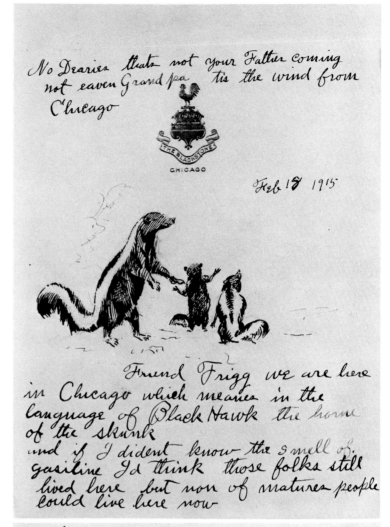

Letter to Friend Trigg, February 18, 1915

Russell's years out of doors had made him acutely conscious of the fumes and odors of a large city. A number of his letters from places like New York and Chicago comment on their unpleasant smells. These were so bad in Chicago that he thought "non of natures people could live there now."

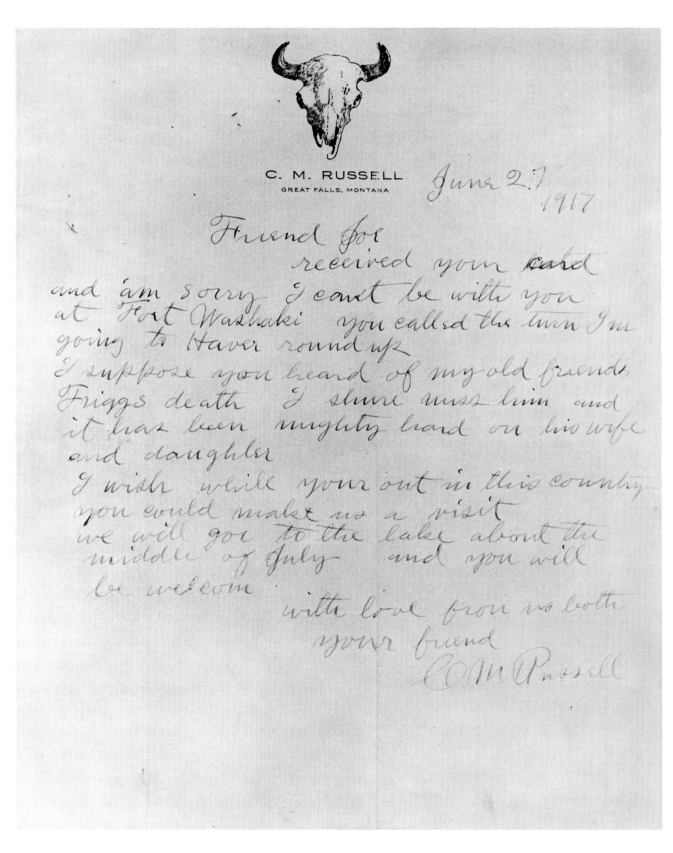

C. M. RUSSELL
GREAT FALLS, MONTANA

June 27 1917

Friend Joe
            received your card
and am sorry I can't be with you
at Fort Washaki you called the turn I'm
going to Haver round up
I suppose you heard of my old friend
Friggs death I shure muss him and
it has been mighty hard on his wife
and daughter
I wish while your out in this country
you could make us a visit
we will goe to the lake about the
middle of July   and you will
be welcom
                    with love from us both
                    your friend
                    CM Russell

Letter to Friend Joe, June 27, 1917.

Joe Scheurle was a young artist from Orange, New Jersey, whom the Russells met on their second trip to New York City in 1905. As the result of the close friendship that developed, the Scheurles made many trips to Montana in later years, staying with the Russells both in Great Falls and at "Bull Head Lodge," their summer cabin on Lake McDonald.

Courtesy of J. Frank Dobie, Austin, Texas

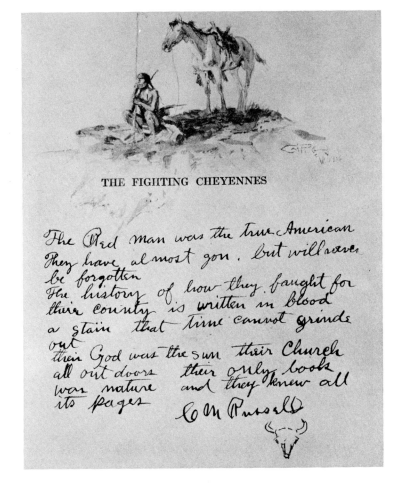

THE FIGHTING CHEYENNES

The Red man was the true American
They have al most gon. but will never
be forgotten
The history of how they faught for
their county is written in blood
a stain that time cannot grinde
out
their God was the sun their Church
all out doors their only book
was nature and they knew all
its pages
                    C M Russell

The Fighting Cheyennes, 1916

Unlike most Montanans of his day, Russell had a deep feeling for the people he called "the true Americans." He admired the Indian's love for their country and the way they lived in harmony with Nature. He respected their customs and was deeply resentful of the deceptive methods members of his own race had used to steal Indian lands. As he once wrote, "I've known some bad Injuns, but for every bad un, I can match 'im with ten whites. Man for man, an Injun's as good as a white man any day. No Injun ever did me dirt an' many a one's done me favors. When he's a good friend, he's the best friend in the world."

Courtesy of the William E. Weiss, Jr., Collection, Whitney Gallery of Western Art, Cody, Wyoming

Photograph of C. M. Russell dressed as an Indian. Courtesy of F. G. Renner, Washington, D. C.

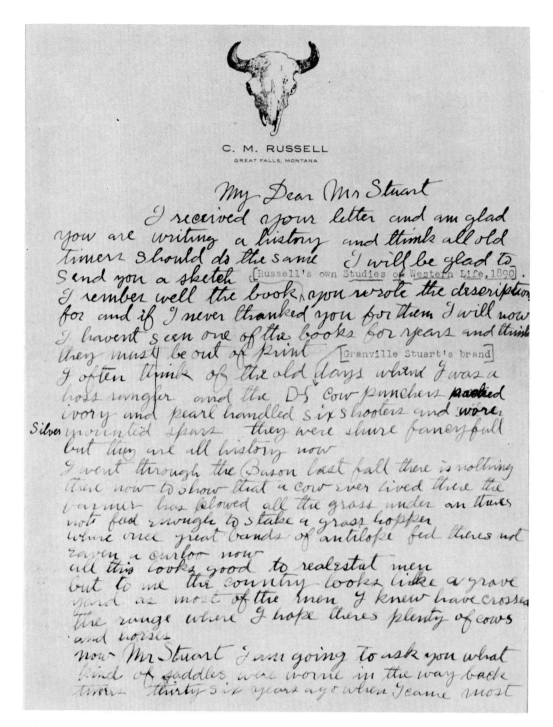

C. M. RUSSELL
GREAT FALLS, MONTANA

My Dear Mr Stuart

I received your letter and am glad you are writing a history and think all old timers should do the same I will be glad to send you a sketch [Russell's own Studies of Western Life, 1890]. I rember well the book you wrote the description for and if I never thanked you for them I will now I havent seen one of the books for years and think they must be out of print [Granville Stuart's brand] I often think of the old days whend I was a hoss wrangler and the DS cow punchers packed ivory and pearl handled six shooters and wore Silver mounted spurs they were shure fancy full but they are all history now

I went through the Basen last fall there is nothing there now to show that a cow ever lived there the farmer has plowed all the grass under an theres not fead enough to stake a grass hopper where once great bands of antilope fed theres not raven a curloo now

all this looks good to realestat men but to me the country looks like a grave yard as most of the men I knew have crossed the range where I hope theres plenty of cows and horses

now Mr Stuart I am going to ask you what kind of saddles were worne in the way back tims thirty six years ago when I came most

Letter to Granville Stuart, undated

One feature that distinguishes Russell's work from that of all other artists who tried to paint the West is accuracy. Whether it was the bead-work on an Indian's moccasins, or the brand on a horse, the observer can be certain such details were exactly as Russell had seen them. Russell's memory was infallible, but if he was planning to paint something he had never seen, he first got the facts, as this inquiry to Granville Stuart indicates.

The "descriptions" mentioned in the accompanying letter were written by Granville Stuart for Russell's first book, a portfolio of his early paintings called *Studies in Western Life,* now one of the exceedingly rare items of Russelliana.

Courtesy of J. Frank Dobie, Austin, Texas

— 68 —

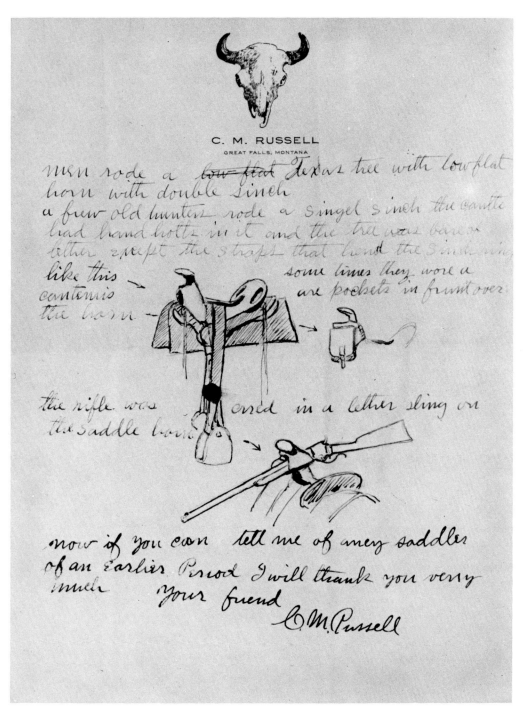

C. M. RUSSELL
GREAT FALLS, MONTANA

Men rode a ~~low flat~~ Texas tree with low flat horn with double sinch

a few old hunters rode a singel sinch the cantle had hand holts in it and the tree was bare or lether except the straps that held the sinch ring

like this → cantinus the horn →

some times they wore a are pockets in frunt over

the rifle was the saddle horn carred in a lether sling on

now if you can tell me of aney saddles of an earlier Period I will thank you very much

Your friend
C. M. Russell

Granville Stuart arrived in Montana in 1857 as a young man, and was to spend the next sixty-one years in the state, becoming one of its most distinguished citizens. The "DHS cowpunchers" mentioned in Russell's letter were those of the Davis-Hauser-Stuart Cattle Company of which Stuart was the manager. The history he was writing appeared as a splendid two-volume work called *Forty Years on the Frontier*. "Nothing better on the cowboy has ever been written" was the way J. Frank Dobie described Stuart's chapter on the cattle business of early-day Montana.

Photograph of Granville Stuart. Courtesy of the Historical Society of Montana, Helena, Montana.

*Letter to Dear Charley (Street)
undated.*

Charles M. Street and Charlie Russell were schoolmates together at the old Tholozan Avenue School in St. Louis before 1880. Charlie, at least, never forgot their teachers. Years later in one of his "Rawhide Rawlins Stories," Russell was to say, "As near as I can remember, them he-school marms we had was made of the same material as a bronco buster. Anyway the one I went to in Missouri had every kid whip-broke. He'd call a name an' pick up a hickory, an' the owner of the name would come tremblin' to the desk."

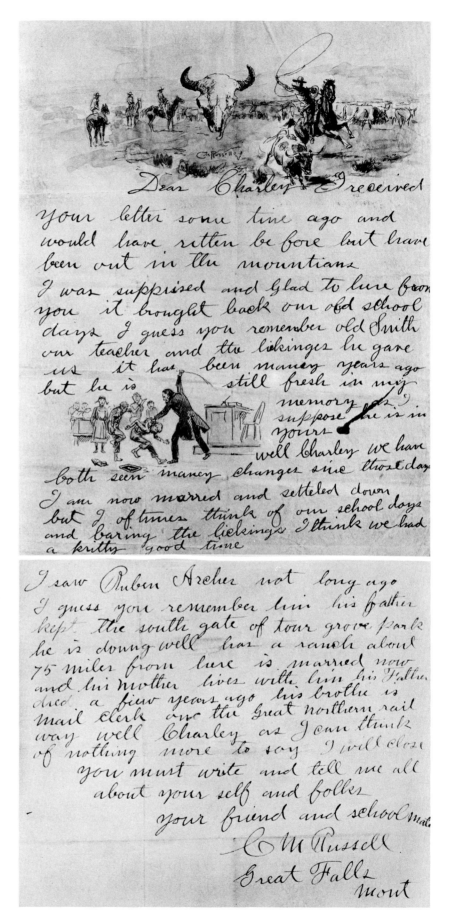

this rider didnt quite win

Jan 28, 1916

Friend Guy I received your letters, an am a little slow about coming back with paper talk. But here goes

I am glad to here you are going to pull another Contest for the folks

Those prizes your hanging up shure look good. But judging from horses and steers you delt out at Calgary and Winnipeg the rider an roper that takes a prize shure had something coming

I have lived among riders most of my life and late years Iv been taking in Contests at different places but yours has got them all skined to the dew claws

An Il take my hat off to eny rider who takes eny tryes to drag a prize from you

An Injun once told me that bravery came from the hart not the head. If my red brother is right Bronk riders and bull dogers are all hart above the wast band but its a good bet theres nothing under there hat but hair

well Guy I hope you get a cross all right and show them Cliff dwelers the real thing

they have all seen wild west shows but yours is no show its a contest where horses and ridirs are strangers

its easy when a bronk twister knows every jump in a hoss but hes ganbling when he steps across one he never saw before You Savy

well Guy I close with best regards to your Self and Wife Your friend

C M Russell

give my regards to Borine and all friends

we will be in New York about the first of March then if you are still in the big camp we talk it over

is Ed Borine still in that owls nest on 42

Letter to Friend Guy Weadick, January 28, 1916

Russell's drawing of the rodeo rider who "didn't quite win" suggests that he hadn't forgotten the magnificent performance Weadick had put on at the first Calgary Stampede four years earlier. With the 1914-1918 war preventing a repeat performance in that city, Russell was delighted to learn that his friend was planning one for the "Cliff Dwellers" of New York City. Misspelling Ed Borein's name and calling his studio in one of New York's tall buildings an "Owl's Nest" was typical of Russell.

The Amon Carter Museum, Fort Worth, Texas

Letter to Ed Borein

Undoubtedly Ed Borein and Charlie Russell would have been close friends no matter when or where they had met. Their lives and tastes were too similar to admit of anything else. Their friendship was especially close because they met in New York. There, surrounded by so much that was strange and so many who were strangers, their common bonds seemed even stronger in contrast. While in New York, Russell was often found in the studio where Borein lived and earned his living as an illustrator. Surrounded by Borein's collection of saddles, boots and other cowboy paraphernalia, the two would cook frijoles and swap stories of the life they knew so well. The studio was on the third floor of a house on West 42nd Street, up several flights of stairs. Russell, who detested the tall buildings of New York, jokingly called it the "Owl's Nest"; but in the "big camp" it was his home.

Courtesy of The Santa Barbara Historical Society, Santa Barbara, California

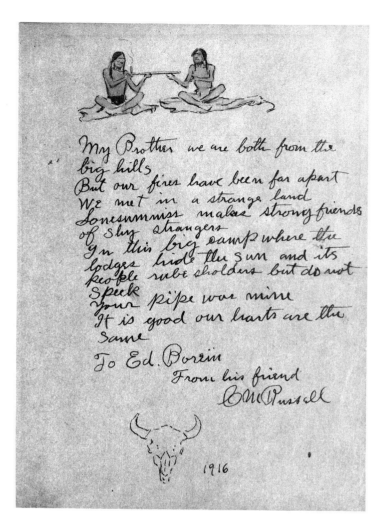

Life Mask of Charles M. Russell ca. 1914. Copyright by The Santa Barbara Historical Society, Santa Barbara, California. Reprinted by special permission of The Santa Barbara Historical Society.

This life mask of Charles M. Russell was made by Ed Borein during one of Charlie's many visits to Borein's New York studio. The mask shows CMR as a man of fifty, with the strong, almost Indian features so familiar in the many photographs and self-portraits of Russell. Because of the process involved in taking the cast, the shock of hair which always fell halfway across Charlie's face had to be brushed back.

Letter to Sid Willis, March 21, 1916

Although the Russells made numerous trips to New York where Nancy was active in promoting the sale of his paintings, Charlie never became used to the "Big Camp," as he called it. The traffic terrified him; the food didn't taste right; and as he put it, "I feel like jumping out of town every time one of those L trains rushes by. It's hard work to dream of hazy foothills and miles of prairie when you hear a new kind of fiendish noise every few minutes. I can't say I relish the whoop of an Indian warrior, but his voice is as sweet as a whip-poor-will compared to the yap of those newsboys."

The Amon Carter Museum,
Fort Worth, Texas

Photograph of Sid Willis. Courtesy of the Great Falls Tribune, Great Falls, Montana.

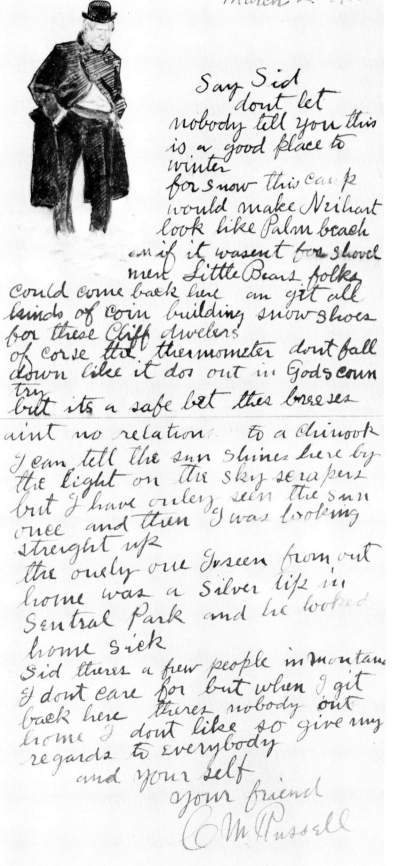

GREAT NORTHERN HOTEL
NEW YORK

March 21 1916

Say Sid dont let nobody tell you this is a good place to winter for snow this camp would make Neihart look like Palm beach an if it wasent for shovel men Little Bears folks could come back here an git all kinds of coin building snow shoes for these Cliff dwelers of corse the thermometer dont fall down like it dos out in Gods coun try but its a safe bet these breeses aint no relation to a chinook I can tell the sun shines here by the light on the sky serapers but I have onley seen the sun once and then I was looking streight up the onely one I seen from out home was a silver tip in Sentral Park and he looked home sick Sid theres a few people in montana I dont care for but when I git back here theres nobody out home I dont like so give my regards to everybody and your self

your friend
C M Russell

— 73 —

GREAT NORTHERN HOTEL
NEW YORK

March 1st
1916

Friend Bill maby you
think this lady is stripped for a bath
but your wrong. Shes at dinner
the evening garments of a female in
this camp wouldent pad a cruch
If clothing is a sign of civilization
an paint spells heathern judging
from she folks here Im among
Savages

Bill I wasent born yesterday and
I knew the old west with the lid
off But the New York Cabaret
has got aney thing Iv ever seen
Skined to a fair you well
Old Davoy Fisky Burnett Masher
Owens eaven Chicago Joe would
have to take there hats off
their Joints would look like the
meeting place of reformers
This town is certainly lively There s
a lot of plungers that usto blow
than coin in France and England
but some how they are gun shy
this yeare nobody cares to go boat
riding So there bunched here
blowing there coin
best regards to yourself
and the bunch
your friend
C M Russell

*Letter to Friend Bill Rance, March 1,
1916*

Although Russell "knew the old west with the
lid off," his letter to Bill Rance suggests a
slight case of shock at the sights he saw on his
first visit to a New York cabaret.

Courtesy of Great Falls, Montana Lodge 214
B. P. O. Elks

C. M. RUSSELL

GREAT FALLS, MONTANA

July 12 1917

C. N. Dickinson

Friend Cris this is the old
horse brands and all
thanking you

your friend

C M Russell

Letter to Friend Chris, July 12, 1917

Russell never generalized in his painting. If he was painting a horse, it was an individual animal he had known that came alive on his canvas or paper. Whether it was the spotted Appaloosa of an Indian or a cowboy's blazed-face sorrel, the animal appeared with the proper markings, even to the brand that identified the present or former owner. Chris Dickinson, Montana rancher turned banker, had asked Charlie for a drawing of Russell's own horse, "Red Bird" and the accompanying letter was his reply.

Courtesy of Bruce Norris, Chicago, Illinois

Letter to Maynard Dixon and Frank Hoffman,
(1917)

When Russell told Maynard Dixon, the California artist, and Frank Hoffman, a New York illustrator, that "the robe will be spread and the pipe lit," he was using the Indian's familiar way of telling friends their visit would be welcome. However, Charlie was probably spoofing when he said "there are no Injuns here." On the subsequent trip, Dixon completed many drawings of the Blackfeet while visiting the Russells at their Bull Head Lodge on Lake McDonald.

Courtesy of Miss Edith Hamlin, San Francisco, California

Charlie Russell's sense of humor expressed itself as often in his drawings as in words. In the little pen and ink and watercolor drawings sent as a Christmas card to Maynard Dixon, the expression on the Indian's face is as irresistable as his message of Christmas cheer.

Courtesy of Miss Edith Hamlin, San Francisco, California

Friend Dixon I received your letter and was glad to here from you

I was at the Winipeg stampede and altho I would like very much to take in Pendleton can afford to this year

we are now at our camp at Lake McDonald and will be here until the twentieth and from then to the thirtieth I will be in Great Falls if you can arrange your dates with these you would be shure glad to see you all at Laton Place

I received the magazines and think your pictures were fine they looked mighty real to me your Indians poneis and lodges were all mighty skookum

I am glad of your success and hope you keep pulling of good things till your light goes out and hope it burns long and bright with out a flicker

I saw some good riding at the stampeed but a good many many of them were unloaded moste of the horses were old out laws from montana and alberta and them twisters had to ride to get the money cause those brouks went high wide and crooked

I have never been to Pendleton but have heard they pull of good riding and roping there and I think it will pay you to go

now Dixon dont forget if you cut my range dont pass my camp

I leave the first of oct for a hunting trip and will be gon about two weeks

with best wishes to you both from my wife and I

your friend C M Russell

PROBABLY JULY OR AUG. 1917

Letter to Friend Dixon, undated, (1917)

Few public affairs had a greater attraction for Russell than a roping and bronco-busting contest. Whether it was a "rodeo" at Havre or Lewistown, Montana, or a "stampede" at Calgary or Winnipeg, Russell could usually be found on the top rail of the corral, renewing acquaintance with his Indian and cowboy friends, or watching the action of the horses he loved.

Courtesy of Miss Edith Hamlin, San Francisco, California

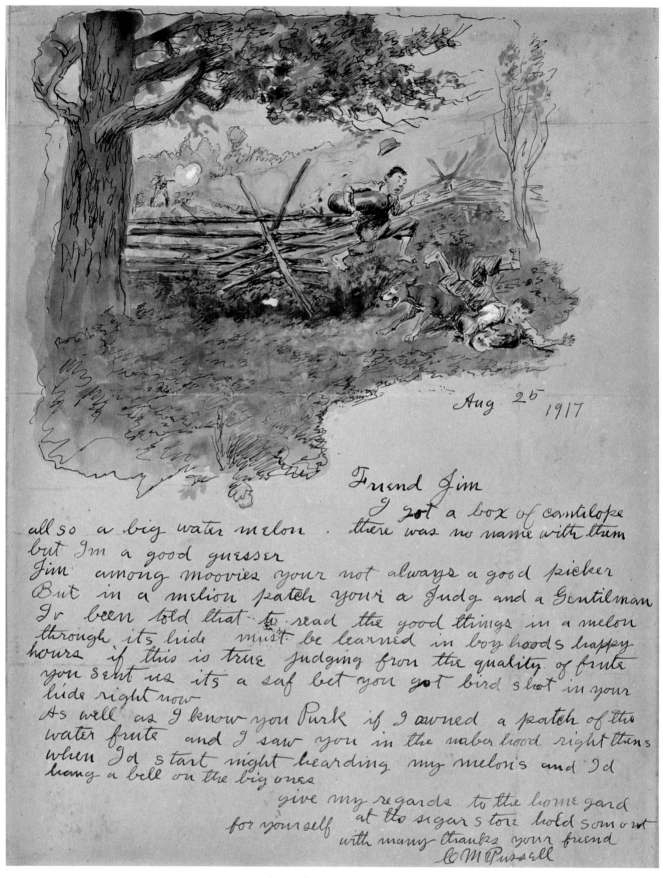

Letter to Friend Jim Perkins, August 25, 1917

As a printer for the old Great Falls *Leader* Charlie's friend Jim Perkins was known as a "one-handed drinking man." This was to distinguish him from most of the other members of his calling who were "two-fisted" in this respect. Jim was also fond of all kinds of melons and when his relatives in Colorado sent him some, they were usually shared with the Russells.

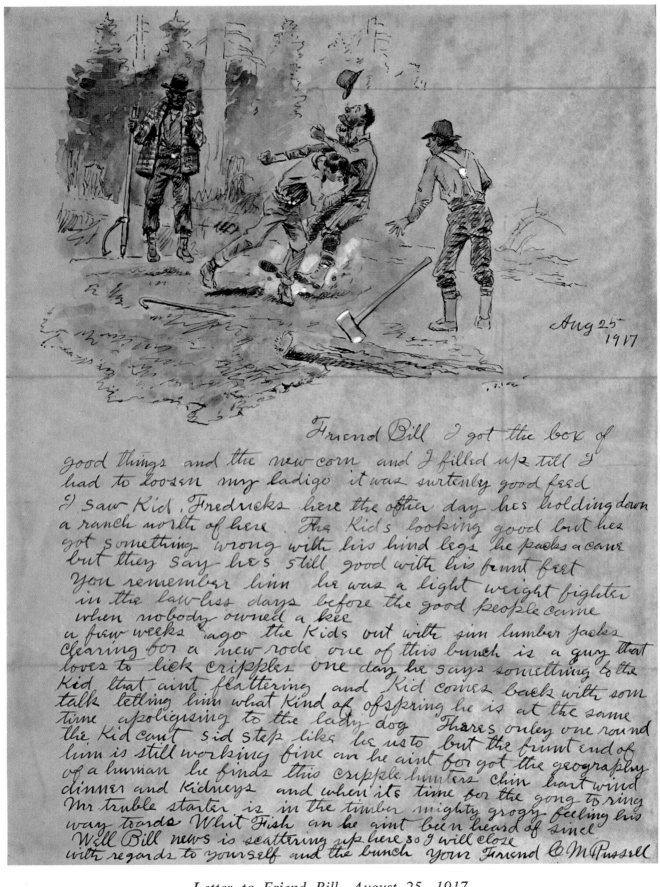

Aug 25
1917

Friend Bill I got the box of
good things and the new corn and I filled up till I
had to loosen my ladigo it was surtenly good feed
I saw Kid Fredricks here the other day hes holding down
a ranch north of here The Kids looking good but hes
got something wrong with his hind legs he packs a cane
but they say hes still good with his frunt feet
You remember him he was a light weight fighter
in the law-less days before the good people came
when nobody owned a kee
a few weeks ago the Kids out with sum lumber jacks
clearing for a new rode one of this bunch is a guy that
loves to lick cripples one day he says something to the
Kid that aint flattering and Kid comes back with som
talk telling him what kind of offspring he is at the same
time apoligising to the lady dog Thares onley one round
the Kid cant sid step like he us to but the frunt end of
him is still working fine an he aint for got the geography
of a human he finds this cripple hunters chin hart wind
dinner and kidneys and when its time for the gong to ring
Mr truble starter is in the timber mighty grogy feeling his
way toards Whit Fish an he aint been heard of since
Well Bill news is scattering up here so I will close
with regards to yourself and the bunch your Friend C M Russell

Letter to Friend Bill, August 25, 1917.

Russell never forgot his wonderful days in Montana before the coming of civilization. He called them "the honest days," with the lid clear off, no laws or restrictions, the latch string always out, and no thievery. This nostalgia was frequently revealed in his letters, as it was here with his reminder to Bill Rance, of "the lawless days before the good people came, when nobody owned a kee."

Courtesy of Great Falls, Montana Lodge 214 B. P. O. Elks

Photograph of Charles Russell and Bill Rance.

Bill Rance, owner of the popular "Silver Dollar" was probably Russell's closest friend among all of the early-day business men of Great Falls. Known for the silver coins embedded in the concrete sidewalk from curb to entrance, the "Silver Dollar" was even more famous than "The Mint" for the fine collection of Russell paintings and illustrated letters that adorned its walls.

Courtesy of "The Mint," Great Falls, Montana

May 7th
1918

Jno L Clark

Dear Sir I received your letter
some time ago in regards to your
carving   there is only one Art Store
here and I know they would be glad
to handle your work but whether they
could sell it I couldent say your work
is like mine many people like to look
at it but there are few buyers
The name of the art store here is the
Como Co Central av
if you send any here I will boost
fore you
I have not ben to the Yellowstone
Park for fifteen years so I can tell you
nothing about it but it might be good
to change your range
if you have an Indian name I
think it would be good to use it
did you ever try modling it seems to me
it would be much easier there is a new
stuff called Modelite that turns hard
when it drys I have used it and think
it good   wishing you good luck
Sincerely C M Russell

Letter to John L. Clark, May 7, 1918

After Russell became well known, many young artists sought his suggestions for ways to improve or help sell their work. Russell was always willing to lend a helping hand, advising them about materials, furnishing the names of dealers or publishers who might be interested, and, most important of all, encouraging them to keep trying. Olaf Seltzer, Joe Scheurle, Will James and John Clark, the recipient of the accompanying letter, were only a few of the struggling young artists Russell helped in this manner.

Courtesy of Dick Flood, Trailside Galleries, Idaho Falls, Idaho

Photograph of John Clark in Indian Headdress.

Courtesy of Dick Flood, Trailside Galleries, Idaho Falls, Idaho

John Clark was a Blackfoot Indian who is best known for his fine wood carvings of Indian chiefs and figures of the grizzly, Rocky Mountain goat, and other animals of his native Montana. The small, hand-colored carvings Clark was selling for a dollar or two at the time of his letter are now eagerly sought by discerning collectors.

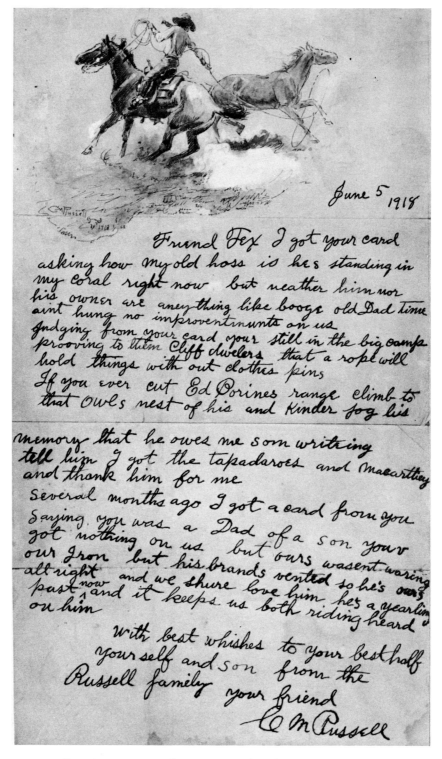

June 5 1918

Friend Tex I got your card asking how my old hoss is hes standing in my coral right now but neather him nor his owner are aneything like booge old Dad time aint hung no improventmunts on us

Judging from your card your still in the big camp prooving to them Cliff dwelers that a rope will hold things with out clothes pins

If you ever cut Ed Borines range climb to that owls nest of his and kinder jog his memory that he owes me som writeing tell him I got the tapadaroes and Macarthey and thank him for me

Several months ago I got a card from you saying you was a Dad of a son your got nothing on us but ours wasent waring our Iron but his brands vented so he's ours all right now and we shure love him hes a yearling past now and it keeps us both riding heard on him

with best whishes to your best half your self and son from the Russell family your friend

C M Russell

Letter to Friend Tex McCloud, June 5, 1918

"Tex" McCloud was the cowboy from San Antonio who won $500 and a saddle for first place in the cowboy's fancy roping contest at the 1912 Calgary Stampede. It is probable that this is where he and Charlie Russell first met. With the passing of the open range, many of Russell's cowboy friends found other, and equally romantic, ways of earning a living. Tex McCloud joined Buffalo Bill's Wild West Show as a trick roper and Will Rogers became a star of Ziegfeld "Follies." Others like Tom Mix, Harry Carey, and Bill Hart helped Hollywood make the first "westerns," while Will James and Ed Borein, and Charlie himself, found success as illustrators and artists.

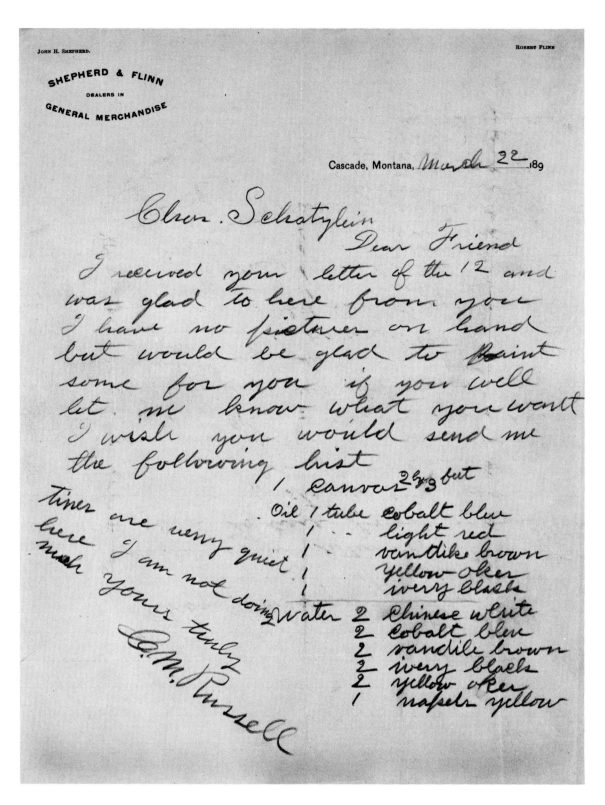

JOHN H. SHEPHERD.

SHEPHERD & FLINN
DEALERS IN
GENERAL MERCHANDISE

ROBERT FLINN

Cascade, Montana, March 22 189

Chas. Schatzlein
        Dear Friend
    I received your letter of the 12 and
was glad to here from you
I have no pictures on hand
but would be glad to paint
some for you if you well
let me know what you want
I wish you would send me
the following list
        1 Canvas 2 by 3 feet
    Oil 1 tube cobalt blue
        1 -- light red
        1 vandike brown
        1 yellow oker
        1 ivery black
Water 2 chinese white
        2 cobalt blue
        2 vandike brown
        2 ivery black
        2 yellow oker
        1 napels yellow

times are very quiet
here I am not doing
much
        Yours truly
        C. M. Russell

Letter to Charles Schatzlein, March 22, 1899.

Charles Schatzlein was the owner of a paint and glass shop in Butte, Montana. In addition to selling Charlie his art supplies, he was the first dealer to promote his work by buying paintings for re-sale. Schatzlein once made a special trip to Great Falls to tell Charlie that reproduction rights on his work were being sold for more than the originals. This was probably the most decisive moment in Charlie's career. Nancy, realizing that her husband would always be diffident about charging a sufficient price for his paintings, appointed herself his business manager, and plugged the leak in the Russell economy by raising prices.

Aug 21 1918

Friend Jim I want to thank you for the good time you gave us at Lethbridge baring that long ride in a short time which was sum scary, we enjoyed every minut.

The above sketch looks like a joke but its a safe bet its going to be history if Big Jim Watson dont quit spuring that gas eater down hill on a loose rain.

Maby noboody'l see it but a fiew Bloods and the cows but they'l have something to tell there grand children.

Now Jim I'v allways been doubtfull about palmistry an dont clame to know trails I aint trailed but if the line on your

front foot called by hand readers the life line is broke in to these palmists are medison men and fortune tellers; its a cinch this dont mean you cash in but your so near across the big range you'l hear harp music mighty plane and the under taker will hang around your camp for quite a while. and when you wake up you'll be looking for a gentle team and a buck board, these hosses will be broke for Grandma the kind that stays in the road your can sit on the ranch an look at the scanry, read the paper or take a nap this sounds mighty slow but you wont be in no hurry,

maby you can find a gentle automobile but I never saw one.

but if your stuck to take chances why dont you try bull doging. it aint so dangeros and theres more glory in it.

of corse a car is easier to throw but it falls so damned hard that the humon gambler takes second money his prize is a wooden over coat with lots of flowers

Letter to Friend Jim, August 21, 1918

Russell might joke about the "scary" automobile ride to Lethbridge from the Alberta ranch of his friend, Jim Watson, but behind his humorous comments he was really serious. Charlie never got used to the automobile, which he called the "White Man's skunk wagon," a machine that "had no branes." He told his wife Nancy, "You can have a car but I'll stick to my hoss; we understand each other better."

The "Hoop up trouble maker" mentioned later in this letter was a concoction of alcohol, chewing tobacco, red pepper, Jamaica ginger and molasses, heated to bring out its full powers, and sold to the Indians as trade whiskey at the old Canadian trading post, Fort Whoop Up.

Courtesy of Jesse Knight, Calgary, Alberta, Canada

Jim you told me that John Bull wants his Injuns to quit out dancing and put in all there time Plowing. Uncle Sam thinks the same it aint my place to give advise to thes old Gents an if Im wrong theirs no harm meant our red brothers aint farmers and never will be but Uncle Sam and John Bull both know that as fighters they aint no push over an if the buffalo came back to morrow theyd be damed hard to get along with they'd raise more hair than theywould wheat why not send there real Americans across to France an get some old time trader to mix up some of that buse they ust to trade at Stand off or troop up let them strip and give them plenty of paint an just before they went over the top

roll out a barrel of hook ups trouble maker bust the head in and tell the red folks its all theires an Im betting when they swarm over on the Kizers men them cheese eaters think sombodys kicked the lid off and all hells loose it will know a new kind of scare in them

I corse there will be a lot of our red brothers that wont draw rations no more but its a cinch them that comes back will be waring german locks on their leggings.

Well Jim as I cant think of any more foolishness I close,

My Wife joins me in wishing you all kinds of luck
and we both thank you again for all your kind ness
your friend
C.M.Russell

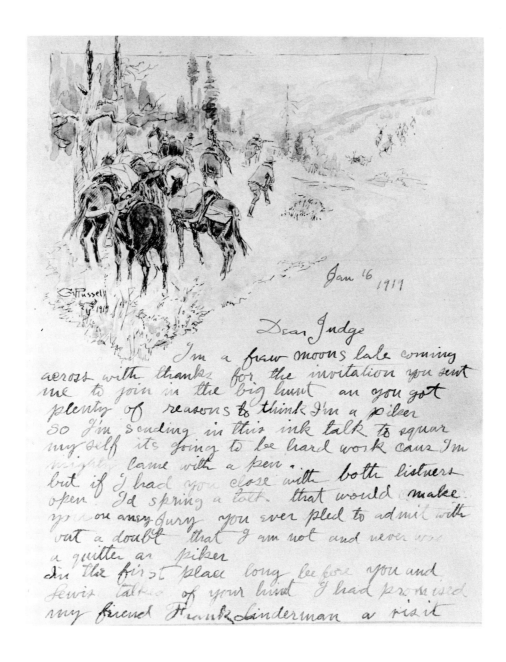

Jan 16 1919

Dear Judge

I'm a few moons late coming
across with thanks for the invitation you sent
me to join in the big hunt an you got
plenty of reasons to think I'm a piker
so I'm sending in this ink talk to squar
my self its going to be hard work caus I'm
mighty lame with a pen.
but if I had you close with both listners
open. I'd spring a talk that would make
you on any jury you ever pled to admit with
out a doubt that I am not and never was
a quitter or piker
In the first place long before you and
Lewis talked of your hunt I had promised
my friend Frank Linderman a visit

LITTLE BEAR
(Chief of the Cree Tribe)

Letter to Dear Judge Bollinger, January 16, 1919

James Bollinger came west in the fall of 1918 for the first of
several annual big-game hunts. He met Russell through his ex-
classmate from Iowa State, John Lewis, who operated the Lewis
Hotel in Glacier National Park. The three men shared a deep
feeling for the out-of-doors and whenever they could arrange it,
the Judge from Davenport, Iowa, the old Northwest fur-trader
turned hotel man, and the artist got together for a fall hunt in the
Montana Rockies.

Loaned anonymously

Photograph of Little Bear with verse by Frank Linderman: Courtesy of the
Log Cabin Studio, Great Falls, Montana

at his camp on Flat Head Lake but I had
called that off and was going to throw in
with the Bolinger and Lewis bunch
then the flew broke out and throws a scare
in me and this old sickness surtenly trimed
this camp hers prutey enough I just sold
a picture to an undertaker
so as long as old flew rode heard on my
camp I didint care to take a long chance
if I went with you to the South fork
I'd be out of reach of letter or wire so I played
safe and went to Lindermans his camp is
right on the road
I stayed with Frank about ten days done som
fishing and had good luck onley hunted three
days saw lots of sign Frank got one
white tail thairs plenty of deer round his
camp but thar shure man wise
I hope you all had good luck I would like
to eat som Elk stake that you cooked
if you're as good with other meat as you are
with beef you aught to write a cook book
you're shure fancey with a frying pan
from Franks cabin I could see your
hunting ground and judging by the
white blanket the Mission range was waring
your camp wasent aney thing like palm Beach
well Judg write and tell me about the hunt
hows Mrs Bolinger and the little boy
I hope we see you all at lake McDonald next
summer give my best regards to all
the Davenport folks thair all marryid
now so I dont know thair names but you
savy the ones I knew at Hoovers camp

my Wife Jack and I whish you all
a Happy New Year
          your friend
          C M Russell
     1219 4 av north
          Great Falls
          Mont

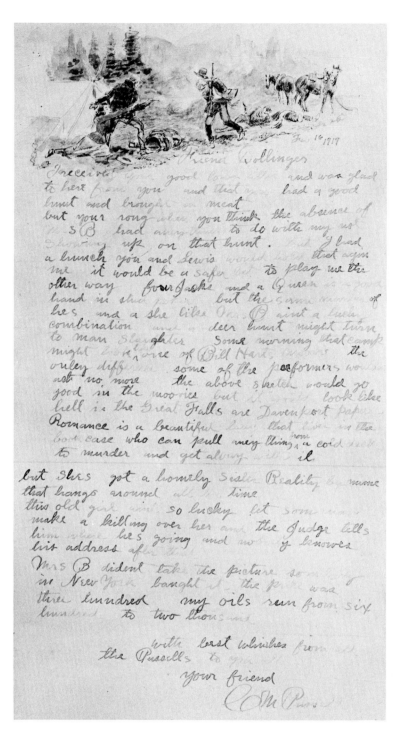

Letter to Friend Bollinger, February 16, 1919.

The year after the accompanying letter was written, Judge Bollinger and Russell were again on a hunting trip in the Rockies with John Lewis. The story is told that the three companions were sitting around the campfire one evening when the subject of religion came into the conversation. Charlie had been quietly listening as the others thoughtfully expressed their opinions and they finally turned to him with questions as to his beliefs. Charlie was rarely at a loss for words in the presence of his close friends, but on this occasion he passed off their inquiry with the remark that "he would let them know later."

Some weeks after they had all returned home, he sent each of his friends his reply — a painting of The Three Wise Men traveling across the star-lit desert to the little town of Bethlehem. The painting shown with the accompanying letter is the one received by Judge Bollinger.

Loaned anonymously

The Three Wise Men, gouache.

The Amon Carter Museum, Fort Worth, Texas

Letter to George W. Farr, March 12, 1919.

One of many interesting side lights of Russell's work is the brands shown on animals. They were true old-time Montana brands which Charlie had seen and remembered. The brand on the saddle horse in the accompanying letter shows that the animal belonged to Alexander Pambrun, owner of the well-known "Rocking P" Ranch on Sun River, an outfit Charlie had worked for in the '90's.

Courtesy of the Historical Society of Montana, Helena, Montana

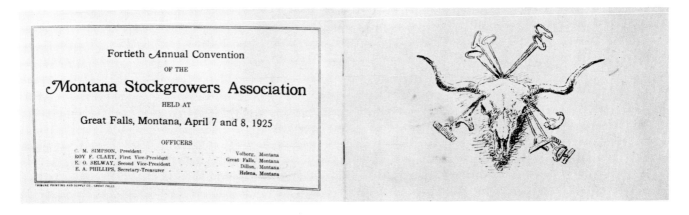

Program of Montana Stockgrowers Meeting, Miles City, Montana.

Courtesy of F. G. Renner, Washington, D. C.

Nothing delighted Charlie Russell more than a chance to visit with old-time Montana cowmen, many of them his friends of an earlier day. He rarely missed the annual meetings of the Montana Stockgrowers Association. The printed programs for these meetings were frequently illustrated with drawings he had made expressly for the purpose.

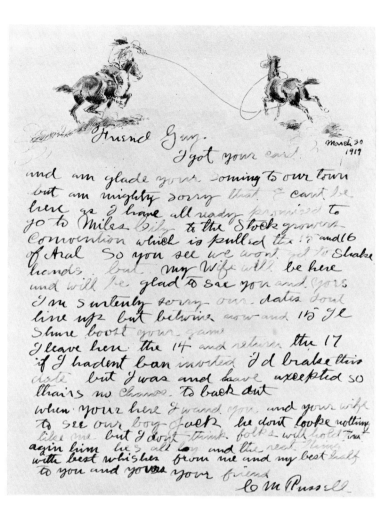

Letter to Guy Weadick, March 30, 1919

The first World War put an end for the time being to the Calgary Stampede, but the show resumed again in 1919 with the celebrated Victory Stampede. Once again CMR had an opportunity to see the splendid riding and roping contests that had so excited him at the first performance. Charlie contributed water-color sketches for the special invitations sent to the Duke of Connaught and to the Prince of Wales. The Prince, now the Duke of Windsor, evidently enjoyed the spectacle; he was a guest at the 1923 Stampede.

"Our boy Jack" mentioned in the accompanying letter had been adopted as a baby three years earlier and Charlie lost few opportunities to tell his friends of his pleasure in his young son. He once wrote, "he's shure a fine boy and loves horses he's got a rocking horse and two stick horses and he rides the tail off the whole string. I still have a couple of cyuses and sometimes I take him in the saddle with me and it shure tickles him."

The Amon Carter Museum, Fort Worth, Texas

Photograph of Charlie and son Jack on Redbird. Courtesy of F. G. Renner, Washington, D.C.

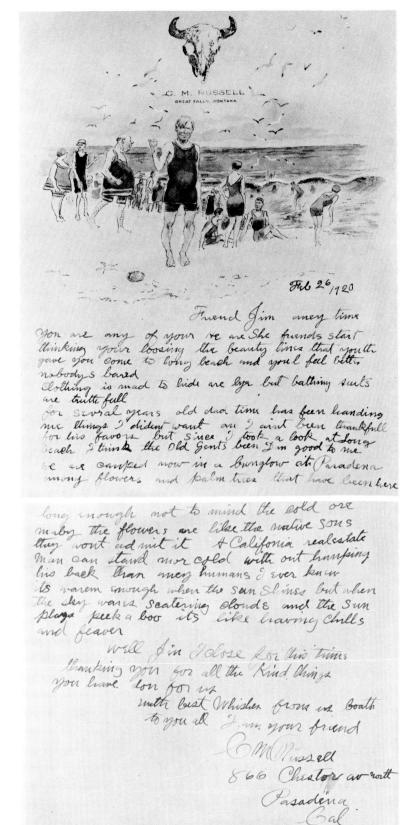

Letter to Friend Jim Hobbins,
February 26, 1920.

Jim Hobbins was Vice President of the Anaconda Copper Company. Charlie's comments about the hardships of a winter in California were probably intended to make the 40 below weather a little more bearable for his friend in Butte, Montana.

The coming of Prohibition meant the end of an era for the famed Mint Bar in Great Falls. Carrie Nation would have found nothing to swing at in the "thirst quenchers" listed on the menu of the "New Mint." In all likelihood, Charlie joined in the mourning for the passing of "the Old Mint." Although he had been a teetotaler for many years before Prohibition came, he was always dubious of attempts to improve morals by legislation.

The Amon Carter Museum, Fort Worth, Texas

The New Mint

SID WILLIS, Prop.

SID'S SPECIALS

DR. PEPPER

Dr. Pepper	5c	Dr. Pepper Nut Sundae	20c
Dr. Pepper Milk Shake	15c	Dr. Pepper Banana Sundae	25c
Dr. Pepper Egg Flip	20c		
Dr. Pepper Malted Milk	25c	Dr. Pepper Pineapple Sundae	25c
Dr. Pepper Egg Malted Milk	30c		
Dr. Pepper Sundae	15c	Dr. Pepper Marshmallow Sundae	20c

Fresh Buttermilk or Sweet Milk with
Whipped Cream 10 Cents

Mint Julep 25c

THIRST QUENCHERS

Root Beer	5c	Loganberry Lemonade	20c
Coco-cola	5c		
Henri-colo	5c	Seltzer Lemonade	20c
Grape Juice	10c	Orangeade	20c
Grape Juice Highball	15c	Lime Freeze	20c
Loganberry	10c	Sparkling Golf Ginger Ale	20c
Loganberry Highball	15c	Lemon Soda	10c
Plain Lemonade	15c	Fresh Buttermilk	10c
Grape Lemonade	20c	Fresh Sweet Milk	10c

PHOSPHATES

Lemon	5	Strawberry	5
Orange	5	Grape	5
Cherry	5	Loganberry	5

PUNCHES

Grenadine Punch	20	Grape Punch	20
Picon Punch	20	Loganberry Punch	20
	Claret Punch	20	

MILK AND EGG DRINKS

Plain Malted Milk all Flavors	20	Egg Chocolate	25
Egg Malted Milk	25	Egg Lemonade	25
		Egg Phosphate	25
Egg Milk Shake	25	Egg Nogg	25

ICE CREAM SODAS

Ice Cream Sodas	15	Plain Ice Cream	10
Chocolate		Vanilla	
Strawberry		Pineapple	
Lemon		Raspberry	
Orange		Maple	

SUNDAES

Plain Sundaes	15	With Nuts	20
Crushed Strawberries	15	Vanilla	20
Crushed Raspberry	15		
Crushed Cherries	15	Maple	20
Crushed Pineapple	15	Chocolate	20

FANCY SUNDAES

Banana Special	30	Whole Walnut	25
Lovers Delight	30	Whole Maraschino	25
	Pineapple Special	30	

MINERAL WATERS

Red Raven	Pluto
	Rock Springs, Etc.	

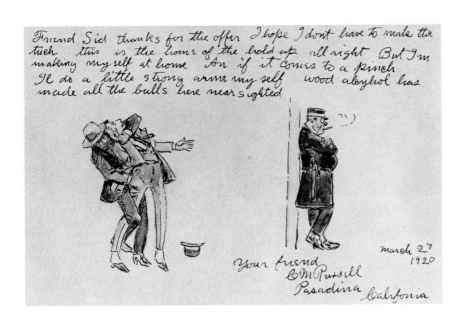

Friend Sid thanks for the offer I hope I dont have to make the
trick this is the home of the hold up all right But I'm
making myself at home An if it comes to a pinch
I'l do a little strong arms my self   wood alcyhol has
made all the bulls here near sighted

Your friend
C M Russell
Pasadina California

march 27
1920

Card to Friend Sid Willis, March 27, 1920.

Photograph of "The Mint"

Courtesy of *"The Mint,"* Great Falls, Montana

When "the Mint" saloon was opened for business in Great Falls, Montana on
August 13, 1898, it boasted the most elegantly appointed place of its kind in the
state, with fixtures of solid mahogany, heavily embossed fresco decorations, and
the richest and most artistic furnishings available. After Sid Willis became the
proprietor about 1908, few visitors to Great Falls failed to see "The Mint" which
was famous for the magnificant collection of paintings, sketches, models, and
other Russell memorabilia its owner had carefully treasured over the years.

As a member of the State Legislature in Montana in 1927, Willis was responsible
for introducing the bill providing for the installation of Russell's statue in the
Nation's Capitol. The installation took place in 1957, thirty years later.

Letter to Robert Thoroughman,
April 14, 1920

Bob Thoroughman embodied both the experiences and skills Russell most admired and Charlie's admiration is reflected in this tribute to his friend. Thoroughman had crossed the Plains with an ox team when he was fifteen, arriving in Virginia City, Montana Territory in 1865. He worked as a cowboy for a number of years, then established his own ranch in Chestnut Valley. Thoroughman was a top-hand as a roper and bronc rider and his likeness appears in many of Russell's paintings of cowboy life.

Note to Robert Thoroughman,
April 14, 1920

Cascade, Montana, the little town twenty miles up-river from Great Falls, had many pleasant associations for Charlie Russell. He had been married there and the surrounding Chestnut Valley was the home of many of the friends he had made during his first years in Montana. Bob Thoroughman was one of these and Charlie always welcomed the chance to visit his friend's ranch and talk over old times.

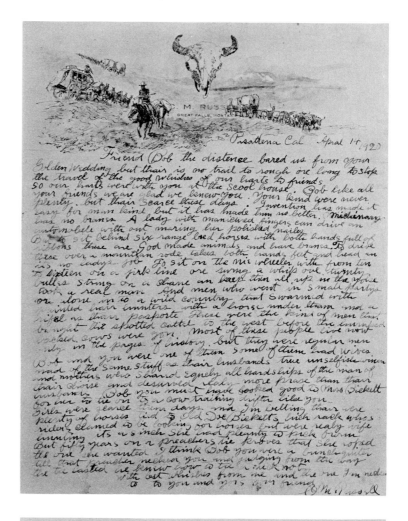

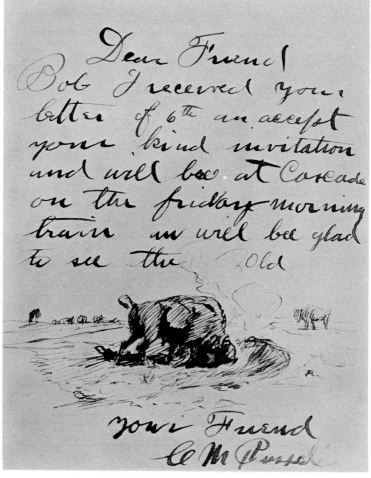

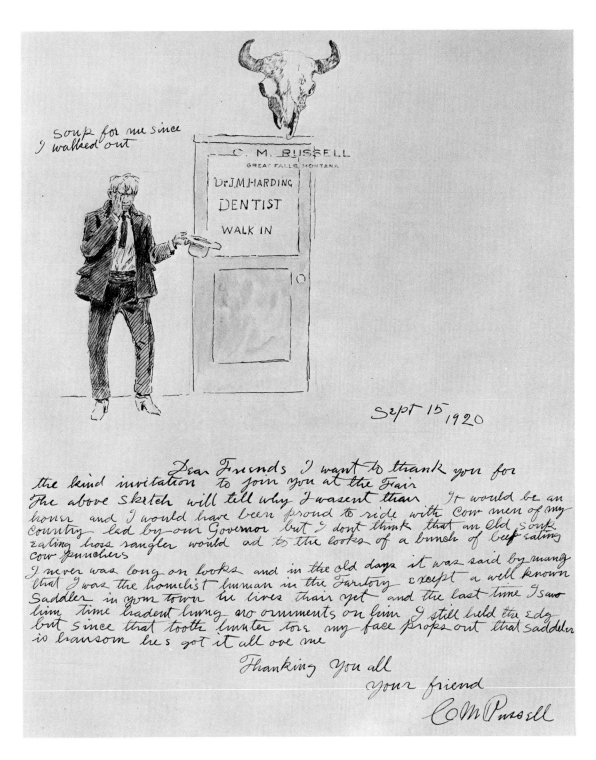

Letter to Friends, September 15, 1920

This letter was written at the beginning of the period of illnesses which marred Charlie's last years. Eventually all of Charlie's teeth had to come out, but, characteristically, he found this situation had its advantages. As he wrote his sister: "When my teeth hurt I take them out an I can sit in a dentist waiting room an read *Life* and laugh at the jokes but I can remember when there wasent a joke in the same block."

The "well known saddler" mentioned in the letter was Ben Roberts, at whose home in Cascade, Montana Charlie had first met Nancy Cooper, his bride-to-be. Russell's reference to his friend's ugliness was part of a playful feud the two men had carried on for thirty years. At their first meeting, Charlie had introduced himself to Roberts, calling him by name. When Ben asked how Charlie happened to know him, his reply was, "Well, they told me when I found a man in Montana as ugly as I was, it would be Ben Roberts."

Courtesy of the Historical Society of Montana

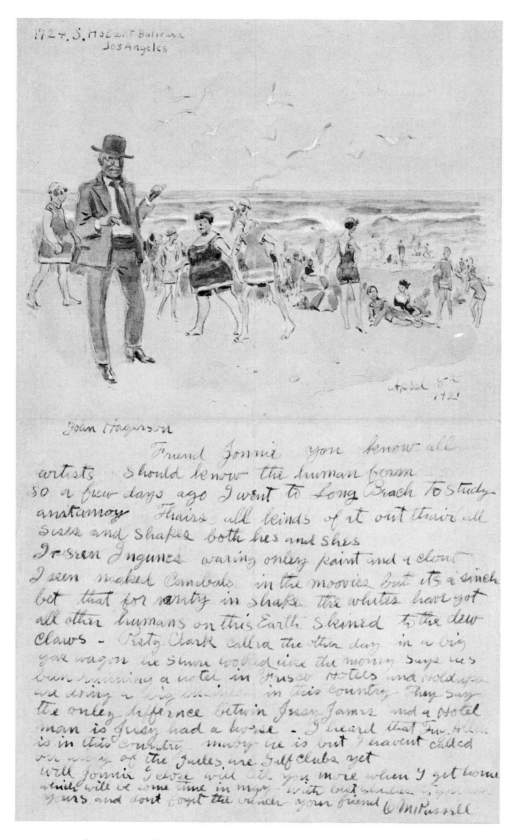

Letter to Friend Jonnie Hagenson, April 8, 1921

When he was fifteen, Charlie attended art school in St. Louis for three days. Drawing from plaster models seemed a waste of time to him, and he never reached an advanced life class. Forty years later, the California beaches gave him his first chance to study anatomy, as he jokingly wrote to John Hagenson, a Great Falls crony. "Thairs all kinds of it out thair — all sizes and shapes both hes and shes." Hagenson owned a cigar store in Great Falls, but Charlie thought a letter care of "The Mint" would reach Hagenson more quickly.

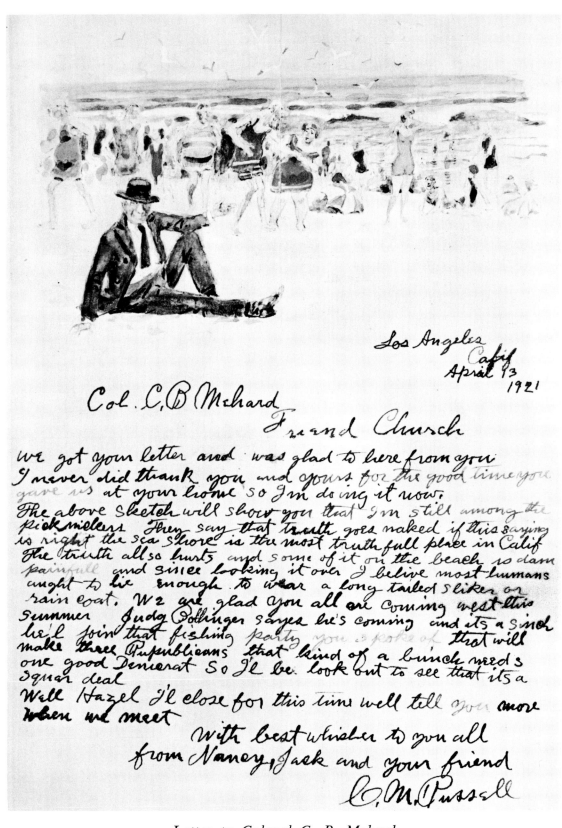

Los Angeles
Calif
April 13
1921

Col. C, B Mehard
Friend Church

we got your letter and was glad to here from you
I never did thank you and yours for the good time you
gave us at your home so I'm doing it now.
The above sketch will show you that I'm still among the
pick nickers They say that truth goes naked if this saying
is right the sea shore is the most truth full place in Calif
The truth allso hurts and some of it on the beach is dam
painfull and sinse looking it over I belive most humans
aught to lie enough to wear a long tailed sliker or
rain coat. We are glad you all are coming west this
Summer Judg Bollinger sayes he's coming and its a sinch
he'l join that fishing party you spoke of that will
make three Republicans that kind of a bunch needs
one good Demicrat So I'l be look out to see that its a
squar deal
Well Hazel I'l close for this time well tell you more
when we meet
                    with best whishes to you all
        from Nancy, Jack and your friend
                                C, M, Russell

Letter to Colonel C. B. Mehard

C. B. Mehard traveled west from Pittsburgh, Pennsylvania to fish with Judge James Bollinger and John Lewis. Russell joined these expeditions whenever he could manage it, because, as he put it "three Republicans like that need a Democrat to keep things equal." It is characteristic of Russell that this joking remark is virtually the only mention of his political affiliations Charlie made. This letter also contains another of CMR's humorous vignettes and descriptions of California beach-life. Charlie's attitude toward the near-nudity he saw on the seashore was by no means disapproval; rather it was amusement at a people who cultivated nakedness with much trouble and expense, while condemning it in savages to whom it was both natural and becoming.

Courtesy of Colonel Harry E. Stewart, Dallas, Texas

Letter to Friend Ed (Borein)
May 1, 1921

California-born Ed Borein was an artist growing up in an era when the old long-horned Spanish cattle and the colorful vaquero were not yet extinct in the state. In his teens he worked the ranches of southern California and sold his first sketches while working as a vaquero on the Jesus Maria Ranch in Santa Barbara county. He met Russell, with whom he had obviously much in common, in New York where Borein worked as an illustrator for many years. The two always kept in touch, especially during the years that both lived in California. Nancy looked upon California as a fertile field for selling her husband's paintings, but Charlie thought more of the opportunity to see Ed Borein, Will Rogers, Charlie Lummis and Leo Carillo, all congenial companions.

Courtesy of the William E. Weiss, Jr., Collection, Whitney Gallery of Western Art, Cody, Wyoming

This photograph of Will Rogers and CMR was made in 1922 at Goldwyn Studios, in front of Stage One during the filming of *A Poor Relation*. The photographer was Clarence Sinclair Bull, for years one of the leading still photographers in Hollywood. He had grown up in Great Falls, Montana, and had met Russell when he was fourteen.

Courtesy of Walt Disney, Burbank, California

Letter to Guy Weadick, November 23, 1921

Forty years ago most westerners were scornful of the easterners who went west for a brief period of "roughing it," while they viewed the scenery. This wasn't true of Russell. With his own deep feeling for the out-of-doors, he understood the need of others to commune with Nature and he respected such friends as Guy Weadick who, as dude ranchers, made such trips possible.

The Amon Carter Museum, Fort Worth, Texas

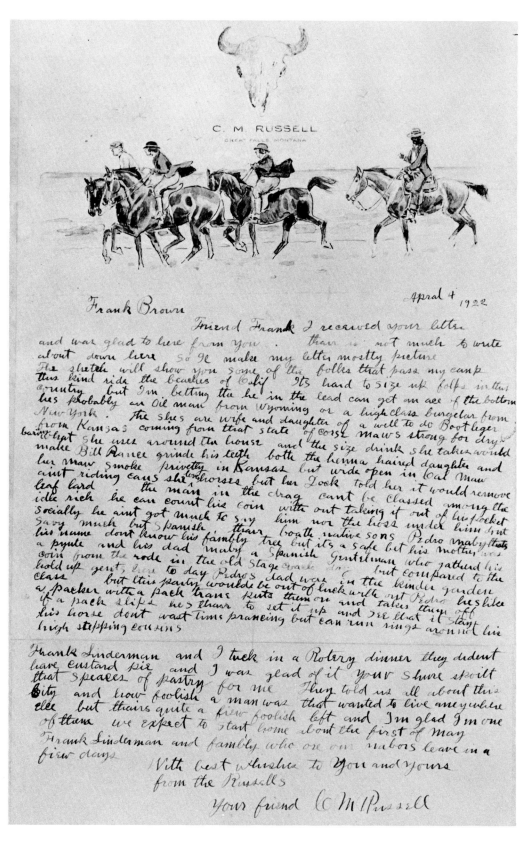

Letter to Frank Brown, April 4, 1922

Charlie Russell was well aware that when he wrote a letter to Great Falls, he was really writing to "most of the folks in Montana." Lucky CMR addressees would pass the letter around for the enjoyment of all. Reading the letter to Frank Brown of the Great Falls Packing Company, about the lady who was trying to get rid of her "leaf lard" was an excuse for "one on the house" at Bill Rance's Silver Dollar Saloon.

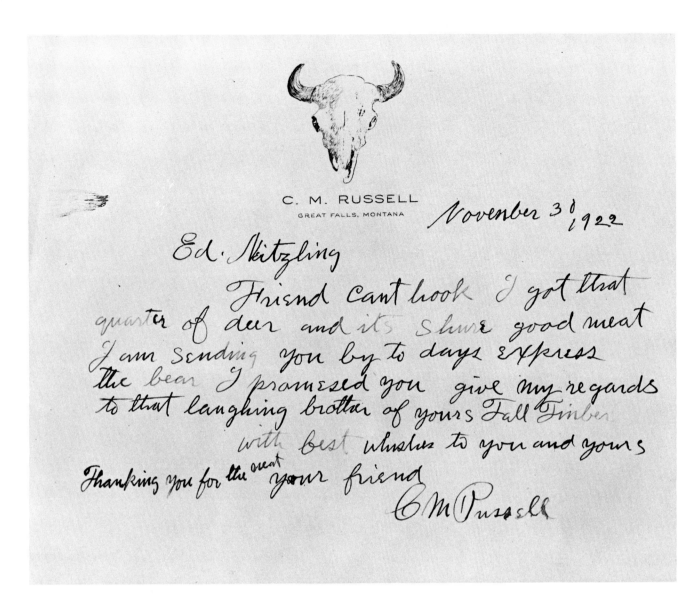

C. M. RUSSELL
GREAT FALLS, MONTANA

November 3⁰/1922

Ed. Nitzling

Friend Cant hook I got that quarter of deer and its shure good meat I am sending you by to days express the bear I promesed you give my regards to that laughing brother of yours Tall Timber

with best wishes to you and yours

Thanking you for the meat

your friend

C M Russell

Letter to Ed Nietzling, November 20, 1922

It amused Russell to invent nicknames for his close friends. The Nietzling brothers were lumberjacks from Kalispel, Montana, so CMR dubbed one "Cant Hook" and the other "Tall Timber." Ed and Charlie were hunting companions of many years standing and 1922 was to see them on their last hunt together. Charlie's rheumatism kept him at home thereafter, but Ed always remembered Charlie's preference for wild meat and sent a hind quarter of venison to the California address. After Charlie's death in 1926, Will Rogers inscribed Ed's copy of *Good Medicine:* "Ed Nietzling. Who packed Charlie and his Dudes in and out. He throws a mean squaw hitch."

The Amon Carter Museum, Fort Worth, Texas

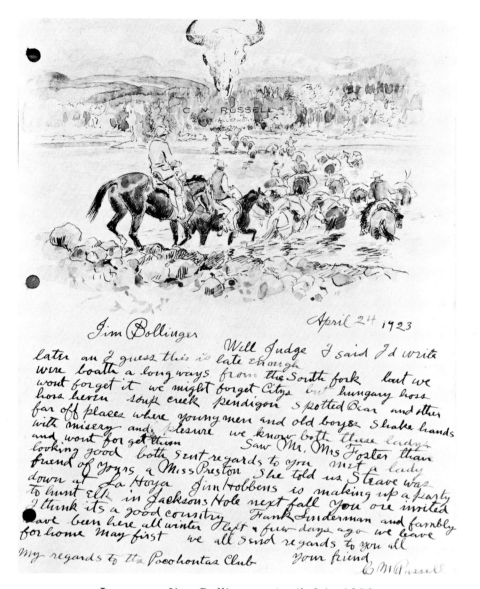

Letter to Jim Bollinger, April 24, 1923

Charles M. Russell and the dignified Judge Bollinger from Davenport, Iowa had many qualities in common. Not the least of these was a love for the open places and the urgent need to get away from the turmoil of the city. Charlie described himself as a "harmless" hunter, but he could not resist the chance to observe again Montana's big game animals in their native haunts, to enjoy his friends and the stories they told around the evening campfire.

Loaned anonymously

Photograph of Judge Bollinger, John Lewis, and C. M. R. Courtesy of F. G. Renner, Washington, D.C.

Letter to George Speck, May 18, 1923

Russell's friend George Speck was a gambling man and Charlie wrote to him in gambling terms. The two men, along with some other out-of-work cowboys, had wintered together in Great Falls in the 90's. Their home was a shack the townspeople had dubbed "The Red Onion." It was George Speck's skill with the paste boards and Charlie's painting that kept the gang in groceries until the grass greened up the following spring.

Their mutual friend "Cut Bank" Brown was another gambler who hailed from Cut Bank, Montana and later became the owner of "The Maverick" in Great Falls.

Courtesy of Dick Flood, Trailside Galleries, Idaho Falls, Idaho

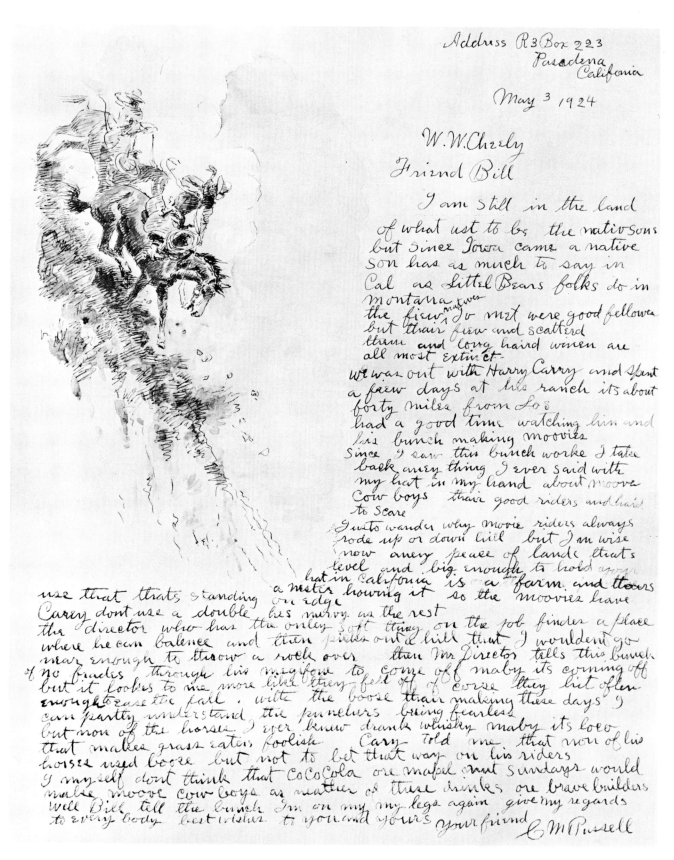

Address R3 Box 223
Pasadena
California

May 3 1924

W.W.Cheely
Friend Bill

I am still in the land
of what ust to be the nativ sons
but since Iowa came a native
son has as much to say in
Cal as Littel Bears folks do in
Montana too
the fiew I met were good fellows
but thair fiew and scatterd
them and long haird wimen are
all most extinct
We was out with Harry Carry and spent
a fiew days at his ranch its about
forty miles from Los
had a good time watching him and
his bunch making moovies
Since I saw this bunch worke I take
back eny thing I ever said with
my hat in my hand about moove
cow boys thair good riders and hard
to scare
I usto wander why movie riders always
rode up or down hill but I'm wise
now eny peace of land thats
level and big enough to hold
a hat in California is a farm and thars
use that thats standing on edge a mister howing it so the moovies have
Carey dont use a double hes nervy on the rest
the director who has the onley soft thing on the job finder a place
where he can balence and then picks out a hill that I woulden go
near enough to throw a rock over then Mr Director tells this bunch
of no brades through his migifone to come off maby its coming off
but it looks to me more like they fell off of corse they hit often
enough to ease the fall. with the boose thair making these days I
can partly understand the punchers bring fearless
but non of the horses I ever knew drank whisky maby its loco
that makes grass eaters foolish Cary told me that non of his
horses used boose but not to bet that way on his riders
I myself dont think that CoCoCola ore mapel nut sundays would
make moove cow boys as nather of these drinks ore brave builders
well Bill tell the bunch Im on my my legs again give my regards
to every body best wishes to you and yours your friend
C M Russell

Letter to W. W. Cheely, May 3, 1924

California was already queen of the movie industry when Charlie began spending his winters there in the twenties. Will Rogers and William S. Hart, friends of long standing, were already at work in films, and through them Charlie met other film cowboys. This letter attests his admiration for Harry Carey who used no stunt man for his dangerous riding shots. Later Russell thought he knew the reason for Carey's courage. "No wonder he aint afraid to ride off them bad hills," he wrote his wife. "After riding with his wife eney thing looks easy." He admitted that Mrs. C. was safe enough in an automobile going straight ahead on a walled-in road with no one else driving that day, but advised Nancy to jump off should she start to reverse.

The Amon Carter Museum, Fort Worth, Texas

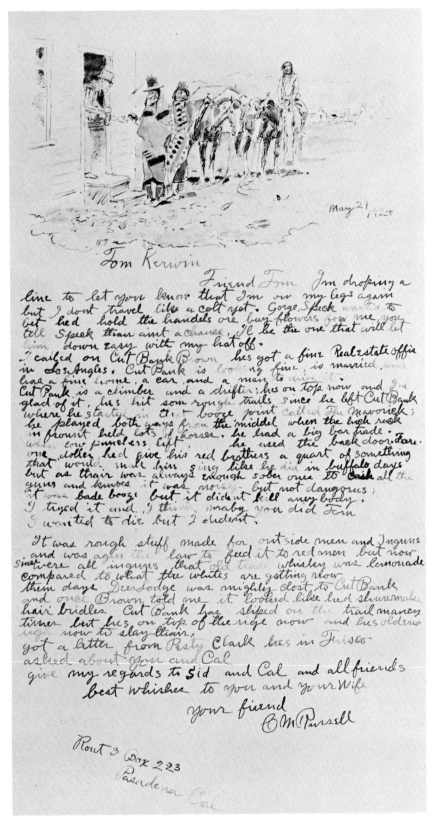

Letter to Tom Kirwin, May 29, 1924

Russell once said, "I had friends when I had nothing else." As long as they were honest it mattered little whether they were cowhands, famous figures from the art or financial worlds, or professional gamblers like Tom Kirwin and George Speck. As tolerant as he was, Charley had little sympathy for those he termed the "morilists." His observation that "now since we're all Injuns" referred to the prohibition laws that made whiskey illegal for the white man, as it had long been for the Indians.

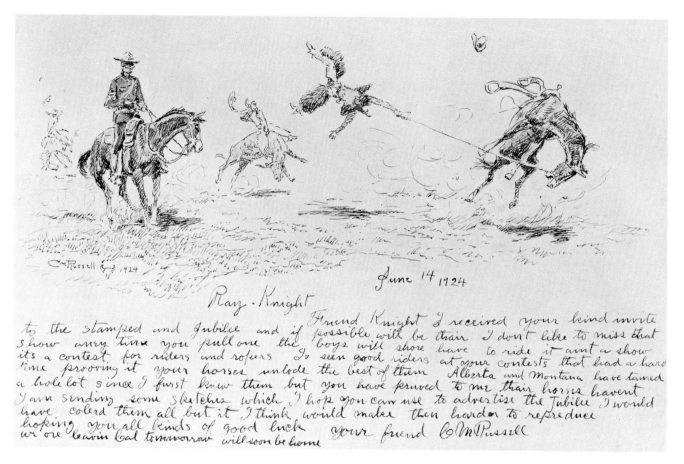

Letter to Ray Knight, June 14, 1924

Raymond Knight migrated from Utah to Canada where he became one of the prominent cowmen of southern Alberta, and in later years was associated with the Calgary Stampede. Although Russell painted many of his friends in his early-day range scenes, Ray Knight has the distinction of being the only modern cowboy to be shown in this manner. The photograph is of a large oil Russell painted of his friend "busting" a steer on his Alberta ranch.

Courtesy of Jesse Knight, Calgary, Alberta, Canada

Photograph: Ray Knight roping a steer. Courtesy of F. G. Renner, Washington, D.C.

*"Christmas Where Women are
Few"*

Courtesy of Chas. S. Jones,
Los Angeles, California

Russell's messages to his friends occasionally took the form of charming verses which were valued as much as his letters. These might be humorous or otherwise, but they usually recalled some incident of the past. "Xmas where Women are Few" tells of the "school marms'" attraction for the women-hungry cowboys of early-day Montana.

Letter to Nancy, December 1, 1924

Charlie Russell was still writing love letters to his devoted wife twenty-eight years after their marriage. The picture he had just finished when he wrote this note was probably "Bruin, Not Bunny, Turned the Leaders," now in the collection of the Gilcrease Institute of American Art, Tulsa, Oklahoma.

The Amon Carter Museum, Fort Worth, Texas

Photograph of Nancy Cooper Russell

Courtesy of "The Mint," Great Falls, Montana

No small part of Russell's success as an artist was due to the efforts of his wife Nancy, or "Mame," as he called her. Nancy sought out prospective purchasers of his paintings, arranged to have the models cast in bronze, and handled all of his business affairs. As Charlie's paintings became better known, Nancy pressed for higher and higher prices. Mrs. Russell became known as "Nancy-the-Robber" among the envious but admiring New York dealers who handled his work. In CMR's words: "Mame's the business end an' I jes' paint. We're pardners. She lives for tomorrow, an' I live for yesterday."

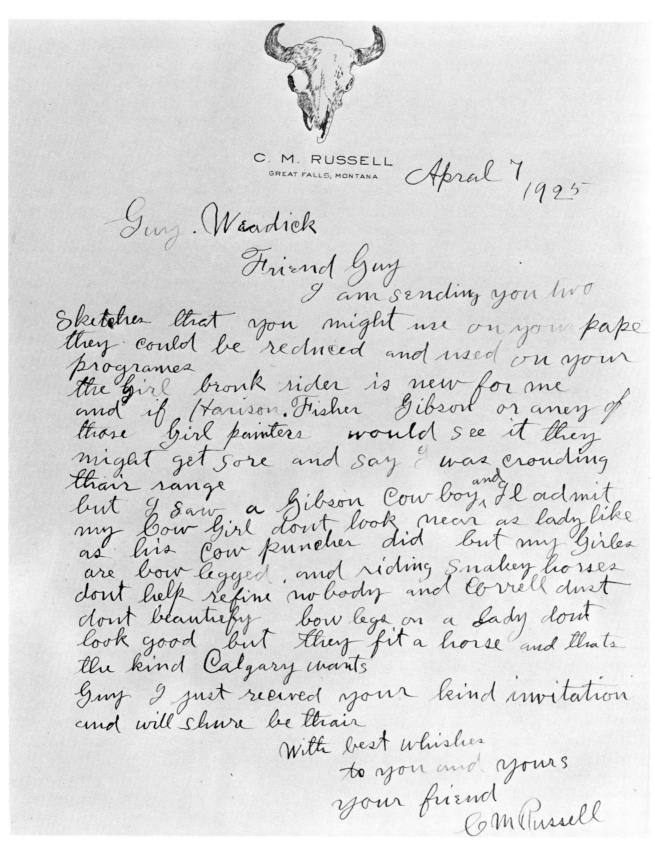

C. M. RUSSELL
GREAT FALLS, MONTANA

Apral 7 1925

Guy. Weadick

Friend Guy

I am sending you two sketches that you might use on your pape they could be reduced and used on your programes the girl bronk rider is new for me and if Harison. Fisher Gibson or aney of those girl painters would see it they might get sore and say I was crouding thair range but I saw a Gibson Cow boy, and I admit my Cow Girl dont look near as lady like as his Cow puncher did but my Girles are bow legged, and riding snakey horses dont help refine nobody and Correll dust dont beautify bow legs on a Lady dont look good but they fit a horse and thats the kind Calgary wants

Guy I just recived your kind invitation and will shure be thair

With best wishes
to you and yours
your friend
C M Russell

Letter to Guy Weadick, April 7, 1925

The sketches accompanying this letter to Guy Weadick were designed as program covers for the Calgary Stampede. Charlie drew this cowgirl as a tribute to the skill of the women contestants at the Stampede. People with "dangerously little" knowledge of Russell's work sometimes state that he never drew or painted a white woman. Nothing could be further from the truth, although in his art men outnumber women as they did in the early West Charlie depicted. An artist as honest as Charlie was would naturally prefer to portray the things he knew best: men, cattle, horses and Indians. The threat he made jokingly to Weadick in this letter of rivaling Harrison Fisher and Charles Dana Gibson, noted illustrators of women, was one he never intended to carry out.

The Amon Carter Museum, Fort Worth, Texas

In 1923 the Prince of Wales, now the Duke of Windsor, was again a guest at the Calgary Stampede. He is shown in this photograph taken at the E. P. Ranch during the 1923 Stampede with the four "cattle kings" of Alberta, the men who sponsored the original Stampede. Left to right: Senator Patrick Burns, George Lane, owner of the Bar U horse and cattle ranch, H. R. H. the Prince of Wales, A. J. McLean, and A. E. Cross. Charlie and Nancy Russell were also guests at this Stampede.

Photograph: Courtesy of Fred Kennedy, Calgary, Alberta, Canada

Watercolors by Charles M. Russell
The Amon Carter Museum, Fort Worth, Texas

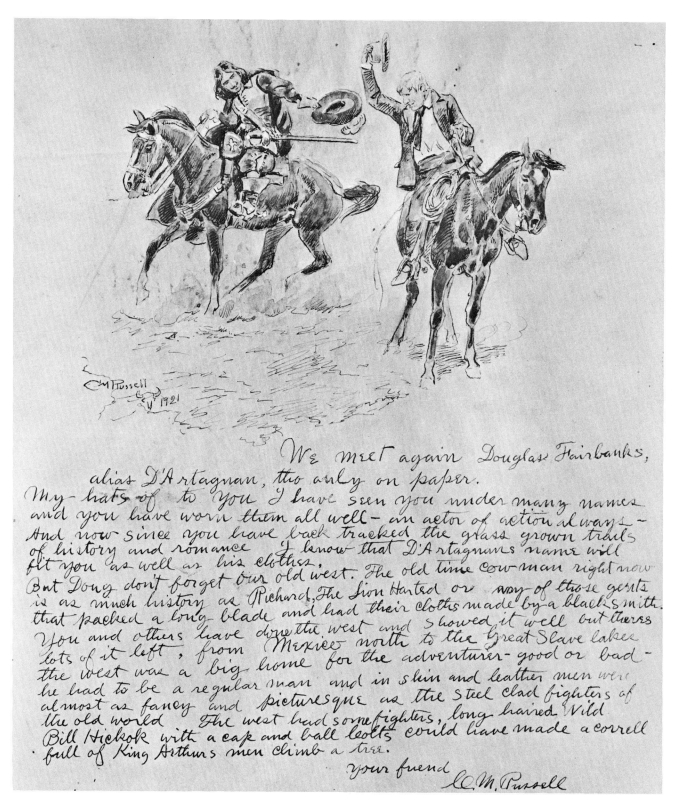

We meet again Douglass Fairbanks,
alias D'Artagnan, tho only on paper.
My hats of to You I have seen you under many names
and you have worn them all well – an actor of action always –
And now since you have back tracked the grass grown trails
of history and romance I know that D'Artagnans name will
fit you as well as his clothes. The old time cow man right now
But Doug don't forget our old west. is as much history as Richard, The Lion Harted or any of those gents
that packed a long blade and had their cloths made by a blacksmith.
You and others have done the west and showed it well but theres
lots of it left, from Mexico north to the Great Slave lakes
the west was a big home for the adventurer – good or bad –
he had to be a regular man and in skin and leather men were
almost as fancy and picturesque as the steel clad fighters of
the old world The west had some fighters, long haired Wild
Bill Hickok with a cap and ball colts could have made a correll
full of King Arthurs men climb a tree.
your friend
C. M. Russell

Letter to Douglas Fairbanks, 1921

One friendship Russell made in the movie colony of the twenties was with Douglas Fairbanks. The story is told that during a dinner party at which both were guests, Fairbanks contributed to the conversation a point-by-point criticism of an equestrian statue owned by their hosts. The others listened in absolute silence. When Fairbanks discovered he had been criticising one of Russell's works, he found it necessary to purchase several thousand dollars' worth of Russell's paintings to get the conversation started again. This incident may explain the graceful obeisance Fairbanks makes in the bronze Charlie modeled of him as d'Artagnan in *The Three Musketeers* — the the most romantic of actors in the most romantic of roles.

Lent by Mr. and Mrs. William H. Bertsche, Jr., Great Falls, Montana

Douglas Fairbanks in the
Role of *D'Artagnan*
Bronze

AMON CARTER MUSEUM
Fort Worth, Texas

Recommendation for Young Boy, Cree Indian, November, 1923

Young Boy, or Mo-See-Ma-Ma-Mos, was a member of a band of wandering Crees. Charlie had met and become friendly with the group in the Judith Basin in 1885. After Russell built his log studio in Great Falls, Young Boy would occasionally drop in to borrow a few dollars with the assurance that he "would pay it back in three moons," a promise that was always kept. More frequently, he would sit for Charlie as a model. His features appear in many of the scenes of an Indian battle or buffalo hunt that Russell painted. Young Boy was the only representative of Russell's Indian friends to attend the artist's funeral, and was the first to visit the Russell home to express his sympathies to Nancy.

The Amon Carter Museum, Fort Worth, Texas

Young Boy, oil painting by Charles M. Russell. Courtesy of John S. du Mont., O.S.J., Greenfield, Massachusetts

Best Wishes, Christmas Card

This Christmas card was sent to Malcolm Mackay of Tenafly, New Jersey who, as a young man left the banking business in New York in search of adventure. He met Russell while working in Montana. In later years, after returning to the family home in the East, the Mackays entertained the Russell's on numerous occasions. On one of these visits, Charlie painted a huge "poster" as he called it, to go over the Mackay fireplace. Known as "Charles M. Russell and His Friends," the painting shows the artist sitting his horse on the brow of a hill with a group of cowboys and a small band of Indians riding out of the canyon toward him. Russell also illustrated, *Cow Range and Hunting Trail,* Mackay's book of his stirring Montana adventures.

Courtesy of the Historical Society of Montana, Helena, Montana

Lithograph, Charles M. Russell and his Friends. Courtesy of the Historical Society of Montana, Helena, Montana

Best wishes for your Christmas
Is all you get from me,
'Cause I aint no Santa Claus —
Don't own no Christmas tree.

But if wishes was health and money,
I'd fill your buck-skin poke,
Your doctor would go hungry
An' you never would be broke.

August 3 1925

John V Potter
          Dear Mr Potter
I have been out in the Mountians
so was late getting your kind
invitiaton I also got one from
Mullens
I am verry sorey but Icant
possibly be at your show
its not bull when I say Im
sorry
Riding and Roping is the only
real American Sport and it takes
regular men to play it
          hoping you all kinds of
luck   and   thanking you
          all
                    Yours C M Russell

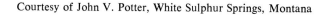

Letter to John V. Potter, August 5, 1925

John Potter was in charge of the rodeo contests planned for Bozeman, Montana in the late summer of 1925 and had invited Russell to attend. CMR declined as he was recovering from an illness, but as always, he contributed this sketch to be used in the Bozeman Roundup publicity.

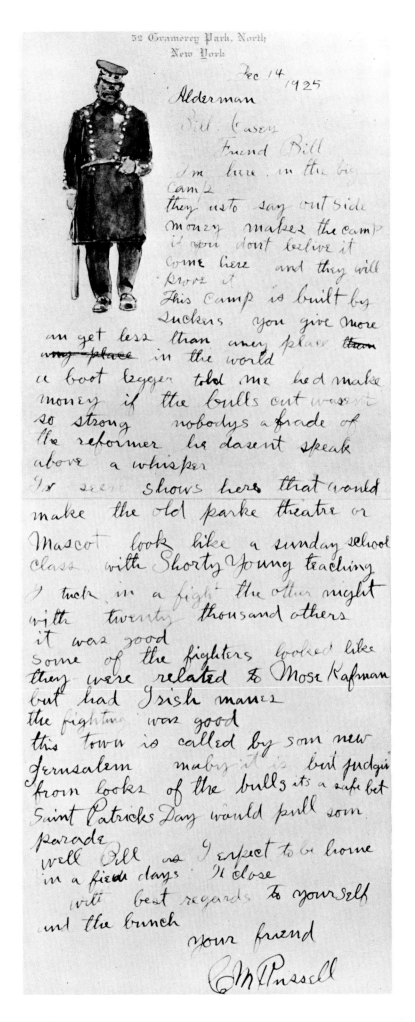

Letter to Alderman Bill Casey,
December 14, 1925

Alderman Bill Casey was one of the men reputed to control the Democratic party in Great Falls but from Charlie's letter, it is obvious that he considered his friends far more conservative than the people and customs he saw in New York. The "old parke theatre" was a burlesque house in Great Falls and Shorty Young, the owner of a honky tonk.

The Amon Carter Museum, Fort Worth, Texas

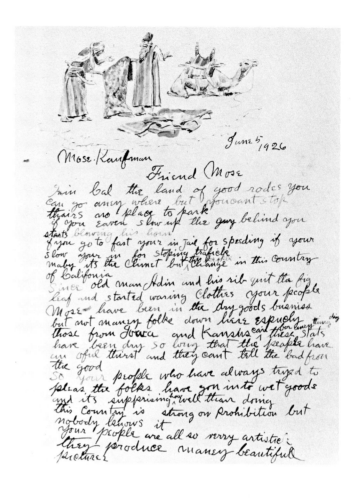

June 5,
1926

Mose Kaufman

Friend Mose

min Cal the land of good rodes you
can go any where but youcant stop
thairs no place to park
if you eaven slow up the guy behind you
starts blowing his horn
if you go to fast your in jail for speeding if your
slow your in for stoping trafick
maby its the climet but things change in this country
of Califonia
Since old man Adin and his rib quit the fig
leaf and started waring Clothes your people
Mose have been in the dry goods busniss
but not many folks down here espucly
those from Iowra and Kansus cant these Stats
have been dry so long that the people have
un oful thirst and they cant tell the bad from
the good
So your people who have always tryd to
pleas the folks have gon into wet goods
and its supprising how well thear doing
this Country is strong on prohibition but
nobody knows it
your people are all so verry artistic
they produce many beautiful
pictures

Mose Kaufman came up the Missouri River in 1880 and after six years at Fort Benton, moved to Great Falls to become one of the town's leading merchants. Kaufman had a great fund of humorous anecdotes about members of his own race and he and Russell were in equal demand as story-tellers with the early residents of Great Falls. Mose admired Charlie's paintings and would sometimes buy one for a few dollars and take it home, only to have Mrs. Kaufman pronounce it "too expensive," and insist that it be returned.

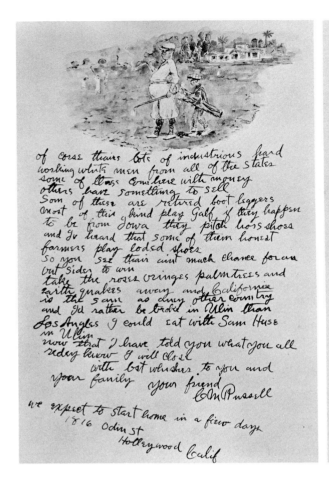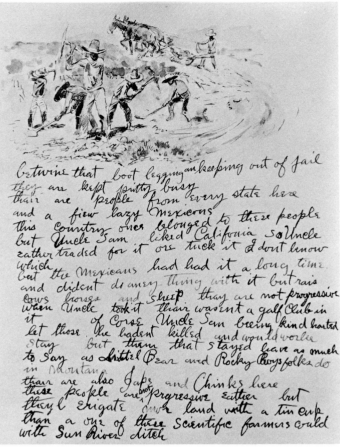

of corse thairs lots of industrious hard
working white men from all of the States
some of those come here with money
others have something to sell
Som of these are retired boot leggers
most of this kind play Galf if they happen
to be from Iowa they pitch hors shoes
and Iv heard that some of them honest
farmers play loded shoes
So you see thair aint much chance for an
out sider to win
take the roses oringes palm trees and
earth quakes away and California
is the same as any other country
and Id rather be broke in Ulm than
Los Angles I could eat with Sam Huse
in Ulm
now that I have told you what you all
reddy know I will close
     with best wishes to you and
your family your friend
          CM Russell
we expect to start home in a few days
1816 Odin st
Hollywood Calif

betwine that boot legging an keeping out of jail
they are kept pritty busy
thair are people from every state here
and a few lazy Mexicans
this country once belonged to these people
but Uncle Sam liked California so Uncle
rather traded for it ore tuck it I dont know
which but the Mexicans had had it a long time
and dident do any thing with it but rais
cows horses and sheep thay are not progressive
when Uncle took it thair wasent a galf Club in
it of corse Uncle Sam beeing kind harted
let those he hadent killed and would worke
stay but them that stayed have as much
to say as Litttel Bear and Rocky Boys folks do
in Montana
thair are also Japs and Chinks here
these people are not progressive eather but
theyl erigate more land with a tin cup
than a one of these scientific farmers could
with Sun River ditch

Letter to Mose Kaufman, June 5, 1926

Mose Kaufman was the proprietor of one of the leading clothing stores in Great Falls. He was well-liked, enjoyed joking, and Russell knew his friend wouldn't mind a little "ribbing" about the California members of Mose's race getting out of the traditional dry-goods business to become purveyors of "wet-goods."

Courtesy of Ira Kaufman, Great Falls, Montana

Heres hoping the worst end of your trail
is behind you
That Dad Time be your friend from
here to the end
And sickness nor sorrow dont
find you

Charlie made this little sketch for our Christmas card this year, and I wish to add my appreciation for the flowers and your sympathetic messages to Jack and me.

Nancy C. Russell

1926 Christmas Card

Like the rest of us, the Russell's sent out a variety of Christmas cards over the years. In the early days these were usually original drawings or watercolors, each one different and made expressly for a particular friend. This became impossible as the number of their friends grew with the years, and the camera was called upon to augment Charlie's pen and brush.

This card was used by Nancy Russell in 1926 the Christmas after Charlie's death. After the pen and ink drawing was completed, Charlie had it photographed and personally hand-colored a small number of prints. These were intended for their closest friends.

Cleatus R. Drake   Marvin D. Evans Company, *Co-Ordinator*

Sal Nasche   Artisan Studio, *Designer*

Fred Clark   Color Associates, *Color Separations*

Marvin D. Evans Company   Printer
Fort Worth, Texas

PAPER TALK is lithographed on 80 lb. Warren's Cameo Brilliant Dull.
Set in Times Roman and Times Roman Italic. Manufactured in the
United States of America.